Steam in England

Steam in England

The Classic Colour Photography of R C Riley
by Rodney Lissenden

with contributions by
Dick Hardy, Nicholas Owen and Christine Riley

Ian Allan
PUBLISHING

FRONT COVER: 'Castle' class 4-6-0 No 5066 *Sir Felix Pole* departing from Swindon on the up 'Cheltenham Spa' express for Paddington on 26 April 1959. The locomotive was ex-works and working back to Old Oak Common, its home shed. Sir Felix Pole was the GWR General Manager between 1921 and 1929.

BACK COVER: The sun sets on the Hayling Island branch as 'Terrier' No 32670 crosses Langston Harbour bridge on a Havant to Hayling Island train on the last day of service, 2 November 1963. The main reason for the closure was the condition of the timber bridge seen here, the cost of a replacement at the time being estimated to be £400,000. The bridge was demolished in 1966, and the stumps of the trestles can clearly be seen today.

HALF TITLE: The Masbury banker hard at work on the Somerset & Dorset, viewed from the brake van on 26 September 1959. Class 3F 0-6-0T No 47557 assists S&D Class 7F 2-8-0 No 53805 on a southbound freight as they climb the Mendip hills to Masbury summit, 811 feet above sea level.

TITLE PAGE: GWR Class 4700 2-8-0 No 4705 departs from Paddington with the 1.25pm to Kingswear, seen passing under Westbourne Park bridge on 27 August 1960. I suspect Dick had a soft spot for this classic class of locomotive!

LEFT: A shed frequently visited by Dick was 73A, Stewarts Lane, where he was always made welcome by the staff. Great pride was taken in the preparation of their locomotives which were rostered to haul well-known named trains. The staff were always willing to move locomotives into a better position for photography; nothing was too much trouble when Dick arrived! Many prints have been passed to those who helped create a better picture. Seen here is BR 'Britannia' class 4-6-2 No 70014 *Iron Duke*, prepared to haul the 'Golden Arrow' from Victoria to Dover Marine, on 24th September 1957.

First published 2009
Reprinted 2009

ISBN 978 0 7110 3388 7

Published by Ian Allan Publishing

an imprint of Ian Allan Publishing Ltd, Hersham Surrey, KT12 4RG
Printed by Ian Allan Printing Ltd, Hersham Surrey, KT12 4RG

Code: 0911/A1

Visit the Ian Allan Publishing website at www.ianallanpublishing.com

Dick spent many happy days on the Somerset & Dorset, often in the company of his friend Ivo Peters. At Evercreech Junction on 6 July 1959, SR 'West Country' class 4-6-2 No 34043 *Combe Martin* heading the down relief to the 'Pines Express', passes No 34044 *Woolacombe* on an up empty stock working.

Introduction

The name R. C. Riley has appeared regularly under photographs in the railway press and on railway books for many years. Known to many as Dick, he took his first black and white photograph in 1937 and when colour film became more available and affordable in 1954, he started to take colour transparencies as well. In this respect, he was very much a pioneer in this field as far as railway photography was concerned. He was the author of 18 railway books covering many of his favourite companies and lines, of which the Great Western was the top of the list, followed by the Brighton section of the Southern.

This book is devoted to Dick's exceptional colour photography. The early transparencies were taken with an Agfa Silette camera with an f3.5 lens and a very slow shutter speed, using Kodachrome 8 ASA film. This severely restricted photography of moving trains and Brian Morrison commented recently that when by the lineside with Dick, he could not understand at the time, why he did not take any action shots! As the equipment improved and Kodak uprated their colour reversal film to 25 ASA, moving trains could be 'stopped' without any problem. Dick remained faithful to Kodachrome 25 ASA film over the years, which has turned out to be a very wise decision, as all these transparencies have retained their colour balance and sharpness, many now over 50 years old.

I felt very privileged when asked to compile this book as a tribute, but little did I realise that the task was so great! The remit was to produce a book of about 250 photographs, the best of the collection covering the Regions of British Railways in England, showing as many locomotive classes and areas as possible. The choice was from over 60 large boxes of slides! The format of the following pages is in proportion with the slides available from the various BR regions and industrial locations, together with the more unusual.

Dick had an excellent relationship with his fellow railway photographers, inspectors, footplate crews and shed staff. He was always ready to help with advice and to provide prints to those who had helped to make a better photograph. It will be noted from the following pages that locomotives were moved, cleaned and a few extra shovels full of coal placed into the firebox to create the right effect. In recent years, a certain inspector was known to give a long whistle when passing Shortlands Junction, with Kent-bound steam specials!

Towards the end of steam on the South Eastern section of the Southern, I spent many hours at the end of Ken Wightman's garden with Ken and Dick photographing the many extra trains bound for the Kent coast resorts. It was long after the end of steam that in 1972, Dick and his wife Christine purchased the house in Albemarle Road, Beckenham, and it was some years later that the gap in the hedge on to the embankment was closed! In later years I spent some good times with Dick seeking help and advice, and often with a request for a specific slide for an RCTS book. Those who were fortunate enough to visit Dick's very full study, were always amazed at his ability to find the print or slide requested within a short space of time. I did not find it so easy sorting the slides however, as enjoyable as it was.

I would like to thank Christine for her help and encouragement in putting these pages together, and to David for his research and specialist knowledge of his father's activities, and to Dick Hardy and Nicholas Owen for writing their personal tributes. I have attempted to make the captions as interesting and informative as possible and I am very grateful to those gentlemen who have checked, corrected and commented in a very helpful way. So my sincere thanks go to Bob Darvill, Dick Hardy, Philip Kelley, Brian Ollett and Dick Taylor. My special thanks to Alan Butcher, Ian Allan Publishing.

Rodney Lissenden
Otford
Kent, July 2009

LEFT: GWR 'King' class 4-6-0 No 6023 *King Edward II* stands at Ranelagh Bridge servicing point in readiness to back down to Paddington to haul the 1.55pm to South Wales on 10 September 1960.

A Celebration

One of the largest gas works in the world, Beckton, in East London, hosted a wonderful array of specially built locomotives, cut down to enable access to much of the site with low clearances. Here, we see one such locomotive, a Neilson 0-4-0WT through the roundhouse arch, on 30 April 1960.

DICK Riley and I had a similar problem, for we were both 'Richard' at home and 'Dick' amongst the railway fraternity, but as this book is a species of monument to both the man and his splendid railway photography, I shall use my discretion! The great thing about Richard was that he was not just a railway enthusiast but also a student of railway affairs. I first met him in the summer of 1955, very soon after I left Stewarts Lane and he had started to take photographs there. I do regret this because we did have special standards of yard and engine cleaning in my time at the Lane, which were never recorded by his camera. He did us justice wherever he went in the Stratford District and, let it be said, we pushed the boat out for him, it was a pleasure to do so. For example, to arrange a footplate pass for him on the Southend road just before the end of steam in 1956. He was quietly very knowledgeable and this appealed to the enginemen and the occasional inspector with whom he rode, so that they usually invited him to come again. This pleased me and I was delighted when he took a close interest in my own job and its many responsibilities, for he listened, he was appreciative and we learned from each other. If the phone rang of an evening at home and it was that calm voice that I came to know so well, there was half an hour gone in a flash to our mutual pleasure.

This interest goes back a long time and here is a story that shows Dick's quality when he was young. In the late 1930s, he and a friend set off for Cardiff to visit Canton depot. The visit had been arranged officially, but they were very anxious to photograph one of the early '29s', *Lady of Lynn*, which was deep in the darkness of the shed. Greatly daring, the two young men went to see the Shedmaster who, after the manner of that hard-pressed breed, happened to burst out of his office and disappear at speed into the distance without a word. However, they persisted and eventually Mr Hughes returned and spoke very kindly to them: 'And what can I do for you young gentlemen?' They were invited into the office and, impressed by their interest and bearing, Mr Hughes had the engine moved outside so that it could be photographed in daylight, and there matters might well have rested.

However, Richard sent Mr Hughes a photograph of *Lady of Lynn* together with the letter of gratitude that means so much to the recipient. By and by, Mr Hughes wrote again saying that, if he made himself known to Driver Bob Roberts at Paddington, he would bring him down from Cardiff General to Canton on the engine. So up Richard went to the engine and there was Mr Roberts with his stiff white collar, white hair and waxed moustache who said: 'Come along at Newport but then if there's nobody about, come and see us at Swindon and you can ride with us through the tunnel.' Imagine what this meant to the young Richard, watching the quiet, ever-vigilant, pipesmoking driver and his middle-aged mate often in vigorous action but with time to explain to Dick a little of the art of firing. Richard never forgot that evening and, what is far more important, he never forgot Mr Hughes and Driver Roberts who became life-long friends to the end of their days.

Syd Norman was the Shop Officeman at Stewarts Lane, very capable in a semi-clerical job which also demanded close contact (usually friendly, but just now and again acrimonious) with his comrades, for he had been a fitter's mate for many years. So Syd was still in overalls but at the Foreman's right hand and he knew everything that was going on, although he was never an informer. He had a comical sense of humour, he could be very sharp, and he was selective about which outsiders he was asked to show around the premises. But he took to Dick at once because he was quiet, civil, friendly, appreciative and knowledgeable. For Syd, apart from being bombed out three times, had worked in the shed since 1919 on just about every class of engine that found its way to Battersea and Stewarts Lane. Richard would ring him up and, so to say, make an appointment for some Sunday morning, off they would go about midday to some unusual place for moving-train photography with a means of access known only to railwaymen who had had to deal with engines in trouble. Maybe Syd would appear in the photograph, standing by the trackside and giving substance to the picture.

We railwaymen loved having our photograph taken beside a much-treasured engine and even against some old crock about which some uproarious yarn could be spun. Dick knew this and was always ready to oblige. I remember when Driver Sammy Gingell retired some two and a half years after I had left the Lane, Dick came down specially to photograph Sam, Fred Pankhurst, the Chief Running

Foreman and me, and so kindly gave us copies, which became family treasures. And there he was again with his camera near Sydenham Hill when we passed by on our way home from Dover. The point is that he got great pleasure from our happiness and appreciation, and his reward was also to know that so many of his pictures are in my treasured albums and always will be.

Dick's knowledge of the history of the steam locomotive was remarkable, a subject that I too studied from childhood. He had his Ahrons, his Burtt and Maskelyne LB&SCR books as I did at the age of seven, so we had much in common. He loved the GWR and I had studied the history of its engines back to the earlier broad-gauge days. We had great enjoyment from this in later life and whereas my knowledge was pretty good, his was profound. How I enjoyed the annual visit to the Stephenson Locomotive Society at Hayes, for we had the time to talk for a couple of hours before Christine produced one of her delectable meals which ensured that I was ready to take on all comers at the meeting. But wherever he went with us on the railway, he was always the same and it was a great pleasure to give him the freedom to explore and also to show him all we could. His writing was a reflection of his personality: interesting, knowledgeable and readable. In *A Night on the Beer and Home with the Milk*, he brought everything and everybody to life, a truly admirable work. He was a great encouragement to me in my writing. We had many points in common, small but important. He liked my long captions which have gradually grown over the years and with experience. They suited my style of writing but when one creates a book of photographs, it is different although it ought not to be because the longer you look at a photograph, the more it should tell you.

Richard was one of that happy band for whom I had arranged footplate experience over many years and who gave me a present in 1982 when I retired. It was a beautiful cut-glass decanter engraved with a 'Britannia' and the words 'Richard Hardy Railwayman 1941 to 1982', and no greater compliment could have been paid me. Those in the room that evening with Gwenda and me were all old friends, some from way back, and Dick was there in full bloom and in his element amongst kindred spirits, not all of whom had met him before, but who were glad to do so and talk to a truly good man.

Richard Hardy

RAILWAYS and journalism have been the great passions of my life. When it comes to a mixture of the two, when I read books and magazines about trains, I have always paid close attention to who has done the writing – and who has taken the photographs. So it was that the name 'R. C. Riley' beside so many fascinating pictures has been a very familiar one to me for many years.

It was not until the early 1990s that I met the man behind the camera. Richard Riley, usually known to his many, many friends as Dick, was obviously a superb photographer. I was quickly captivated, too, by his tremendously wide knowledge of all railway matters. It was also clear straight away that he was the nicest of men, eager always to share his love and enthusiasm for this endlessly fascinating subject.

This book, rightly, pays tribute in the main to Dick's faultless skills in capturing steam engines in all their many glories. What delighted me about him was the way he embraced all sorts of trains, including my beloved Southern electrics. Thanks to R. C. Riley's pictures, I got to know many locations, whether London termini, or in the suburbs, or in the lovely southern countryside and at the seaside, long before actually going to them.

And getting to know him meant learning so much delicious detail about the trains, the stations, and the lines he shot. If I had to choose a favourite scene, it would be the long procession of new Kent-coast stock drawn up on one line of the Ardingly branch before going into service in 1959.

Steam fanatics won't mind, I'm sure, if I say that one of my earliest meetings with him had nothing to do with trains. He and I went with another good and long-standing friend, Tony Dyer, to a bus rally. Dick was soon snapping away, and talking knowledgeably about the 'RTs', the 'Routemasters', and the rest.

For the truth is that all transport interested him. In later years, the house in Beckenham where he and Christine lived had Eurostars passing the back garden. Dick was fascinated by them, even though they made quite a racket compared with the soothing hum and subdued clatter of the Southern services.

It was such a pleasure to go to the house, to enjoy the Rileys' hospitality, and to go into the upstairs room piled from floor to ceiling with railway books. How the floorboards took the weight, I cannot imagine. So many of the books had Riley pictures in them. Some, of course, he had authored. It seemed to me that every book ever written about trains since about 1930 was there somewhere.

SR 'Remembrance' class 4-6-0 No 32331 *Beattie*. This class was built by the London, Brighton & South Coast Railway as 4-6-4 tank engines. The Southern Railway rebuilt the whole class of seven, between 1934 and 1936 as 4-6-0 tender locomotives. Seen on 23 June 1957 near Dick's home in Tulse Hill, *Beattie* hauls a ramblers' excursion, the 'Riverside Special' to Windsor for the Runnymede Rally.

For instance, after he died, Christine kindly suggested I take a couple. One was *I Drove the Cheltenham Flyer*, a gripping account of the pre-war days when the Great Western put on some thrillingly fast services. It was a little early for Dick to have any photos in it. But I bet, like me, he loved the book.

As Christine has observed, he was involved in many groups and causes. Both the Railway Heritage Trust and the Heritage Railway Association benefited enormously from having him as an adviser. One of his great pleasures was to be a judge for the National Railway Heritage Awards.

When it comes to individual lines, Dick had an especially close relationship almost from its inception five decades ago with the Bluebell, in Sussex. He not only provided vital historical information and advice; several items of equipment, from engine parts to signal gear, were donated by him, as this, the first of so many preserved railways, developed.

I was so glad to be able to speak publicly about Dick late in 2008 when digging began to get rid of a huge rubbish tip standing between the Bluebell's northernmost point and the planned extension to East Grinstead. How pleased he would be to see that dream accomplished.

Only a month before his death, Dick and I enjoyed a marvellous evening together. That great railwayman Chris Green gave a lecture at the London School of Economics to the Railway Study Association to mark the centenary of John Betjeman's birth. Betjeman was a hero to Dick, and the two had actually met. That made Dick a celebrity at the RSA meeting. Even though he was quite frail, he took the microphone to recall memories of the much-loved poet.

Dick was a great photographer, and a wonderful friend. Even though he is so much missed, his work will always live on, as these subsequent pages demonstrate so eloquently.

Nicholas Owen

LMS Class 3F 0-6-0 No 43584 gets the road and sets off on a down freight, on 12 April 1958. This scene at Burton-on-Trent, shows a fine array of lower quadrant signals and a busy yard in the distance.

Richard, the family man behind the camera

ABOVE: Dick had a real love for the Bluebell Railway and was involved from the beginning, having some influence on the preservation of the North London Railway 0-6-0 tank and then the Adams Radial 4-4-2T. In the early days of operation, on 26 May 1963, SECR 'P' class 0-6-0T No 27 and Brighton 'Terrier' 0-6-0T No 55 *Stepney* await the right of way from Sheffield Park.

MANY times I have sat at the typewriter to type captions and introductions to the numerous books to which Richard put his name. Never did I fully understand the extent of his memory, writing ability or passion for his subject as I have come to realise during the production of this book. I only ever saw the near-end result of his labours, but was always aware of his attention to detail and accuracy. He will be remembered for many things, not least by other aspiring authors and enthusiasts who sought his help. His time, expertise and historical knowledge were always available to others, and he freely gave all three to those who approached him.

Richard and I were married in 1965 and our two sons, David and Philip, were born in 1966 and 1968. Just as steam was coming to a close on the British main line his attention and time were now needed elsewhere. Throughout their childhood he would seize upon every opportunity to pursue his photography and, as his children will testify, we covered most of the preserved railways – the preferred holiday destinations! However, the serious photography and active participation were mostly curtailed to meet the demands of a young family and their education. It was not until 1978 that the offer of early retirement from the banking world became a reality and it meant that once again he had the time to pursue his great passions – books, writing and everything connected with the world of railways. He was fortunate to have been involved as a consultant to the National Railway Museum during its early years in York under the direction of his great friend John Coiley. This helped to bridge the gap between fulltime employment and retirement, and he thoroughly enjoyed the experience and all that it offered him.

Looking at his very first book, *Great Western Album*, I am amazed to see that the publication date was 1966, the year our elder son was born. Other books were produced during those early years, which Richard always maintained kept him at home as distinct from being at the lineside! During 1971, a book was compiled entitled *Railway History in Pictures, The West Country*. On looking through it recently I discovered mention of Bernard Moore's 'Travelling',

RIGHT: The Adams Radial tank, No 488, leaves Sheffield Park on the Bluebell Railway on 22 June 1974. This locomotive has an amazing tale of survival: built for the LSWR by Neilson & Co in 1885, sold to the Ministry of Munitions in World War One, purchased by the East Kent Railway where it remained until 1946 when £800 was paid by the Southern Railway for it. The 4-4-2T joined the two remaining locomotives of the class ('0415') to work the restricted Lyme Regis branch. British Railways withdrew No 30583, as it had become under BR numbering, in July 1961. It was promptly purchased by the Bluebell, where it has seen many years use, but is currently awaiting an overhaul. Dick was a historical adviser to the ARPS and his son David recalls the visit of Captain Peter Manisty and his father, to see Horace May, then general manager of the Bluebell Railway, to discuss the benefits to the railway and the nation as a whole, if this locomotive could be preserved. Mr May was finally persuaded that it should be saved, thanks to Dick's negotiating skills!

A very happy shot of Dick Riley on the occasion of a trip around Kent on the 'Queen of Scots' vintage train, 25 July 1999. Wondering how to get home from Headcorn to Shortlands, his great friend Inspector Colin Kerswell, suggested a cab ride on Class 73 electro-diesel No 73101; not a hard decision to make! *Brian Stephenson*

extracted from *A Cornish Chorus*. Quite by coincidence this poem was read at the time of the scattering of Richard's ashes on the Bluebell Railway in October 2006.

Once he had retired he was able to devote much time to his beloved books. Anyone who visited our home will recall the enormous library and archival material he had amassed over the years, and it is only in the time since his death that I have fully appreciated the huge subject range that was within that library. He adored books and they were among his most treasured possessions. Our two sons were brought up to share the same respect, and I recall his great pride when his elder granddaughter, Caitlin – aged three or four at the time – showed huge disgust on discovering that a children's storybook had been defaced by another young child.

David and Philip were a huge pride to him, as were his two granddaughters. Philip recalls being very impressed when his father was asked to supply a photograph of an engine carrying the nameplate *Manchester United* for the football club's museum. Philip's passion at the time was first-division football as distinct from railways! However, David shared his father's passion for steam and they undertook many nostalgic trips together. One such outing was behind *Sir Nigel Gresley* from Carnforth to Ravenglass and others behind *Tangmere* in more recent years, both locomotives becoming firm favourites. They also loved to visit the Bluebell Railway together,

and David recalls his father's pace seeming to quicken when within the sound and smell of steam.

At Horsted Keynes they would make for his favourite bench and be utterly contented just watching the various locomotives coming and going. The same shared passion extended to listening to the many memories of Richard growing up in a different era, his professional experiences within the banking world, namely Glyn, Mills & Co (later to become part of the RBS Group). However, it was many of his wartime memories which particularly fascinated David and left him speechless. Richard had joined the Royal Engineers in 1943 and later went into Railway Operating. This meant time spent at the Longmoor Military Railway, later transferring to Normandy where he helped to restore railways in northern France, Belgium and Holland. He eventually ended up at the HQ of the Dutch Railways in Utrecht where he was issued with a first-class pass and a pass to travel on the footplate; no marks for guessing which was used most frequently!

Often described as a gentleman, Richard was also a gentle man and this was confirmed in a frequently told story about his time in Belgium. His one shot fired in anger occurred when he disturbed an intruder attempting to steal coal from the yard. Needless to say this was fired into the air. During his later years Richard maintained his interests in a variety of ways. He was a member of 46 different societies, attending many meetings and events. One of his great annual joys was being a judge in the 'Best Kept Station' Awards, which took him to a variety of interesting destinations throughout the southeast. Richard's family was very important to him. If ever advice or support were needed by the immediate or extended family, his wisdom and integrity could always be relied upon.

I should like to thank all those who have helped in the production of this book, particularly Peter Waller for his advice and encouragement, and David for his unbelievable recall of so many anecdotes passed on to him by his father. However, it is to Rodney Lissenden that I express enormous gratitude for his endless time, energy and friendship, not only in the compilation of this book, but throughout the time since Richard's death. Without his constant help and support in the disposal of the vast collection, the Riley family would still be floundering. We miss Richard very much, not just as a husband, father and grandfather, but for his love, friendship and profound wisdom.

Christine Riley

ABOVE: A real illustration of pollution! Although local accommodation was much sought after by the railway enthusiast, one wonders how the residents living by Ranelagh Bridge depot coped with the constant smoke, smell and noise. GWR 'King' class 4-6-0 No 6006 *King George I* is turned on the turntable, 30 March 1957.

The former GWR shed at St Philip's Marsh, Bristol, with the autumn sunlight shining through the glass roof on 9 October 1963.

Western Region

LEFT: 'King' class 4-6-0 No 6025 *King Henry III* and 'Castle' class 4-6-0 No 5058 *Earl of Clancarty* await the right of way at Newton Abbot on a Paddington to Penzance train. The date is 14 July 1955, so this is one of Dick's earliest colour transparencies; a safe station location as Kodak 8 ASA film was not fast enough for moving trains!

ABOVE: Old Oak Common shed always made a real effort to supply clean engines for the race day specials to Newbury Racecourse station. On 5 March 1960 we see 'Castle' class 4-6-0 No 5074 *Hampden* having arrived from Paddington and left its train to turn on the turntable. No 5074 was originally named *Denbigh Castle* but was renamed after the World War Two RAF bomber aircraft in January 1941, to celebrate the Battle of Britain. Also in view is 'King' class 4-6-0 No 6010 *King Charles I* at the head of the 'Members' First Class Special', the most prestigious of the race day workings.

Fresh from overhaul, 'Castle' class 4-6-0 No 5049 *Earl of Plymouth* stands at Swindon shed, being prepared for the road by the shed driver, on 6 September 1959. No 5049 was built at Swindon in 1936 at a cost of £5,800, running more than 1¼ million miles before being withdrawn from St Philip's Marsh, Bristol in March 1963.

A beautiful portrait in perfect light of 'Castle' class 4-6-0 No 7017 *G. J. Churchward* at Old Oak Common shed on 29 August 1959. George Jackson Churchward was born on 31 January 1857, and became the Chief Mechanical Engineer of the Great Western Railway from 1902 until 1922. He was killed on 19 December 1933 when struck by an express train while casually inspecting a defective sleeper on the track at Swindon. The engine named after him was built in August 1948; the nameplates were removed after it had been in service for a few days but were replaced for a naming ceremony on 29 October 1948. Unusually, the smokebox numberplate was cast in brass when the locomotive was built.

Great Western 'Hall' class 4-6-0 No 5959 *Mawley Hall,* built at Swindon and entered traffic in January 1936. Looking very smart in British Railways lined-black livery at Old Oak Common shed in late 1956.

In the 1950s and early 1960s, Swindon Works and shed were visited fairly regularly by Dick. Most Sundays the whole area was opened to the public and in late morning queues would form outside the works entrance with many enthusiasts eager to record and photograph the locomotives on site. Ex-works 'Modified Hall' class 4-6-0 No 6989 *Wightwick Hall*, built at Swindon in March 1948, is seen in the shed on 13 May 1961. Today, it is undergoing a lengthy restoration at the Buckinghamshire Railway Centre.

G. J. Churchward designed the very handsome '4700' class of 2-8-0s, of which only nine were built at Swindon, and introduced to traffic in 1919. They were specially designed for fast freight, but in British Railways days seven were painted in full passenger lined-green and enjoyed a spell of use on passenger turns.

No 4705 stands at Laira shed, Plymouth on 25 September 1960. Withdrawal took place in 1963. This engine was derailed at Stratton St Margaret in November 1954 after running into the buffer stops, the driver having misread the signal.

LEFT: 'Castle' class 4-6-0 No 7023 *Penrice Castle*, built by British Railways at Swindon Works in June 1949 to Collett's Great Western design. Seen emerging from Colwall Tunnel at Malvern Wells, on the line between Hereford and Worcester, it heads the up 'Cathedrals Express' to Paddington on 18 August 1962. The actual castle was a ruin on the Gower Peninsula, 11 miles south west of Swansea. The 'Cathedrals Express' name was introduced in 1957.

ABOVE: The Riley family spent many happy summer holidays at Teignmouth and Dawlish; no doubt Dick had some influence on the locations of those holidays! 'Castle' class 4-6-0 No 5055 *Earl of Eldon* is captured at speed on the up 'Devonian' express on 14 July 1959. The church in Teignmouth can be seen in the background. The sea wall along this part of the coast has always been a Mecca for photographers. No 5055 was built at Swindon Works in June 1936 and was withdrawn in September 1964.

GWR 'Grange' class 4-6-0 No 6824 *Ashley Grange* stands outside the shed at Penzance on 24 September 1960. The class of 80 locomotives was built at Swindon as Lot No 308 between 1936 and 1939. This name is of particular interest as it was once the home of cricketer W. G. Grace, in Ashley Down Road, Bristol. The building was demolished in 1936 and the last of the class was withdrawn in 1965. None survived, but the 81st locomotive, No 6880 *Betton Grange,* is currently under construction on the Llangollen Railway.

The visits to Swindon nearly always produced several ex-works locomotives awaiting return to traffic. Resplendent after overhaul, 'Manor' class 4-6-0 No 7827 *Lydham Manor* stands in the works yard on 16 August 1959. The first batch of 20 'Manors' was built at Swindon in 1938/9 while the final ten were completed in 1950, after the war and Nationalisation. They were built for the lighter lines, known as the blue routes. No 7827 was withdrawn from service in 1965 and sent to Woodham Brothers at Barry for scrap, but was purchased by the Dart Valley Railway Association in 1970 for preservation, and can be seen today on the Paignton & Dartmouth Steam Railway.

One of the early batch of GWR '4900' 'Hall' class 4-6-0s, No 4909 *Blakesley Hall* is seen near West London Sidings, heading the 2.35pm Paddington to Weston-super-Mare service on 13 August 1960. It was built at Swindon and entered traffic in January 1929, named after the hall in Yardley, Birmingham, which is now part of the Birmingham Museum & Art Gallery. No 4909 was withdrawn in September 1962.

The last Chief Mechanical Engineer of the GWR, F. W. Hawksworth, who took office in 1941, produced one completely new tender engine design, the 'County' '1000' class 4-6-0s which appeared in 1945. No 1009 *County of Carmarthen* at Tiverton Junction on the 4.30pm Taunton to Newton Abbot service on 15 June 1962. It appeared in traffic in December 1945, was named in February 1948, and withdrawn from service in February 1963. None of the class of 30 survived the cutter's torch, but a replica 'County' is being built at Didcot Railway Centre, to be numbered 1014 and named *County of Glamorgan*.

'Modified Hall' '6959' class 4-6-0 No 6974 *Bryngwyn Hall,* named after a building north of Tremeirchion, near Mold, Clwyd, entered service two months before Nationalisation in January 1948. Hawksworth introduced the 'Modified Halls' in 1944. This is a scene full of interest on 18 April 1956 as the 5.35pm to Paddington awaits the road and a GWR diesel railcar approaches the station at Oxford.

GWR 'Hall' class 4-6-0 5976 *Ashwicke Hall* heads the down 'Royal Duchy' express, the 1.30pm Paddington to Penzance service, at Hungerford on 4 July 1959. This locomotive was built at Swindon to a Collett design entering traffic in September 1938. In total, 258 'Halls' were built at Swindon between 1928 and 1943. No 5976 was withdrawn in July 1964.

A 'Grange' and a 'Modified Hall', Nos 6855 *Saighton Grange* and 6988 *Swithland Hall,* pass Stonecombe sidings on the down 'Cornish Riviera'. On summer Saturdays, the train was usually worked by a 'King' from Paddington to Newton Abbot where a pair of 4-6-0s worked forward, fast to Truro. The quarry at Stonecombe supplied ballast for permanent way work on the Great Western and was protected by a rather austere signalbox. Dick obviously spent some time at this location on 19 July 1958. His records state that the photograph was taken at 1/250 of a second at an aperture of f2.5.

A 'Manor' in full cry at Tilehurst! Only just over two years before withdrawal No 7808 *Cookham Manor* heads west on an express from Paddington. Dick spent the summer Saturday of 27 July 1963 in the area of Tilehurst and Goring, his records showing that between 11am and 4.30pm he saw 37 diesel and 39 steam-hauled trains. With the price of film, not all were recorded by the camera. No 7808 is preserved at the Didcot Railway Centre.

Another Sunday visit to Swindon Works on 16 June 1957. GWR '4300' class 2-6-0 No 4358 stands in the yard after attention in the works. Built at Swindon to a Churchward design, no fewer than 342 locomotives of this class were erected between 1911 and 1932. A batch built during the First World War was painted in unlined khaki livery and, at the time of writing, No 5322 preserved at Didcot, is turned out in this livery. By Nationalisation in 1948, the class had reduced to 241 locomotives, No 4358 was withdrawn in August 1959.

GWR '4300' class 2-6-0 No 6372 resplendent in lined green livery, specially cleaned for railtour duty on 8 July 1956, stands in the shed yard at Andover. The RCTS ran the 'Wessex Wyvern' tour from Waterloo to Southampton, Ringwood, Dorchester, Isle of Portland, Yeovil, Trowbridge, Savernake and Andover, returning to Waterloo, a total of 334 miles. The Society arranged a variety of motive power: 'Schools' class 4-4-0 No 30925 *Cheltenham* worked to Brockenhurst, 'T9' class 4-4-0 No 30287 to Weymouth, Great Western tank No 1368 performed on the Weymouth Quay branch and No 4624 worked on to the Isle of Portland. The locomotive illustrated headed the special from Weymouth to Andover while the last SR 'Remembrance' class 4-6-0, No 32329 *Stephenson,* made its final run, on the last leg, into Waterloo.

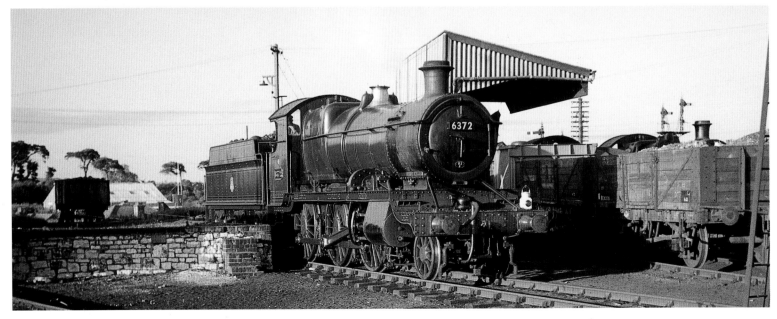

Churchward '4300' class 2-6-0 7306 leaves Barnstaple Junction on the 10.40am to Taunton on 20 July 1964. From Dick's excellent records we know that the shed roof had recently been removed and that the diesel shunter was No D3522.

He also comments: '7306 made a fine sight making its way up and over the river viaduct with strident exhaust'.

Introduced in 1893 by Dean for the Great Western Railway, '2301' class 0-6-0 No 2516 awaits its fate at Swindon on 5 November 1960. Fortunately, No 2516 was not scrapped but was restored and placed on display at the Great Western Railway Museum at Swindon, when it was opened in 1962, along with 'Star' class 4-6-0 No 4003 *Lode Star* and '9400' class 0-6-0PT No 9400.

The Great Western '2251' class or 'Collett Goods' 0-6-0 was a type more generally known for work on rural branch goods and cross country passenger services. No 2253 was photographed at Old Oak Common shed on 16 August 1959, when its duties were reduced to local trip workings in the London area. The third locomotive of the class to be built at Swindon, in March 1930, No 2253 was withdrawn in March 1965, its final years being served at Worcester shed.

On foreign ground, '2251' class 0-6-0 No 2214 enters Southampton Terminus, having worked down the Didcot, Newbury & Southampton line via Winchester Chesil from Didcot. A very interesting scene captured on 26 June 1957, with a varied selection of liveries of former LSWR and GWR rolling stock.

The mainstay of heavy freight power on the Great Western was the fleet of '28XX' 2-8-0s, a design which dated back to 1903. These engines were notable as the first 2-8-0s in the country, and apart from superheating, the basic design underwent only minor alterations in half a century. Here we see No 3864, from the last batch of the '2884' class, built in 1942, heading a down freight at Cowley Bridge Junction, Exeter on 16 July 1958. The wartime-built locomotives originally had solid cab sides, but windows were added from 1946 onwards.

A peaceful picture of a typical Great Western station. Grampound Road was situated between St Austell and Truro on the broad gauge line, opened on 4 May 1859 and converted to standard gauge in 1892. The station opened in 1889 and closed to all traffic in 1964.

Saltash, with Brunel's Royal Albert bridge over the River Tamar, photographed on 12 July 1955, before the road bridge was built. An auto-train crosses the bridge on the service to Plymouth. The bridge was opened in May 1859 by Prince Albert, but sadly, Brunel was too ill to attend the ceremony, and he died on 15 September 1859. The 150th anniversary of the opening of the bridge was commemorated in 2009.

Another peaceful view; Grafton station on the Midland & South Western Junction Railway, on 8 July 1956. The line which ran between Swindon, Marlborough and Andover was opened in 1882 and was closed in 1961.

Thorverton station on the Great Western line between Stoke Canon and Tiverton, opened in 1885 and closed to passenger traffic on 7 October 1963, and completely on 4 May 1964. This view was taken on 3 July 1963.

ABOVE LEFT: Hawksworth's short wheelbase '1500' class outside-cylinder 0-6-0PTs were introduced in 1949 for heavy shunting. The class of ten locomotives was built under BR auspices and entered traffic with smokebox numberplates. All were built in the year of introduction. No 1505 was photographed at Old Oak Common shed on 20 May 1956, where its main duties were empty stock workings in and out of Paddington.

LEFT: Another of Dick's very early colour transparencies illustrates one of the few '5700' class 0-6-0PTs to be painted in mixed traffic lined black. No 8763 is seen at Old Oak Common shed on 28 November 1954. It was built at Swindon Works in 1933, one of a class of 863 locomotives built over a period of 28 years, the most numerous class on the Great Western Railway.

ABOVE: A small class of 11 condensing locomotives was built at Swindon in 1933 to replace older locomotives of the '63' class. They were built for work over the Metropolitan line to Smithfield and were also found in and around Old Oak Common shunting and working empty stock into and out of Paddington. No 9704, with an 81A, Old Oak Common shedplate, gives the location of the photograph dated 28 November 1954. Withdrawal took place in December 1963.

Built during the Second World War, '5700' class 0-6-0PT No 9605 stands in the station at Swindon, on 26 April 1959. A number of the class were sold by BR to the National Coal Board for work in South Wales collieries, and to London Transport for permanent way work in and around the Capital. No 9605 was withdrawn in September 1965.

Class 4200 2-8-0T No 4273 stands at St Blazey shed on 20 July 1960. The type was originally designed for work in the South Wales coalfield, with its short but heavy hauls between pit and port or factory. No 4273 entered traffic in March 1920 and after some years in the valleys moved to St Blazey to work china clay trains around Par and Fowey. Many of the class were withdrawn when the traffic in South Wales was dieselised in the early 1960s.

The GWR 2-6-2Ts of Classes 3150, 5101 and 6100 were built over the period 1903 to 1949, a real tribute to Churchward's practice of producing a single prototype and giving it a thorough tryout before building in numbers. During 1938, a start was made on the reconstruction of the 41 engines of the '3150' class as Collett's '3101' design. The old frames were used but new boilers and smaller wheels were fitted. No 3101, seen outside the shed at Stratford upon Avon, was rebuilt from No 3156 in February 1939, and was withdrawn in September 1957.

LEFT: Emerging from Parson's Tunnel, between Dawlish and Teignmouth, '5101' class 2-6-2T No 4117 heads a local train from Exeter to Newton Abbot, past Parson's & Clerk signalbox on 14 July 1959. In 1954, this class was represented at 31 Western Region sheds, which gives a good picture of the activities of the type – principally passenger work in all areas other than the London Division, which was the stronghold of the '6100' class. No 4117 entered traffic in November 1936 and was withdrawn in September 1961.

ABOVE RIGHT: A scene at Acton West Junction on 30 June 1956 as '6100' class 2-6-2T No 6123 heads west on a local from Paddington as condensing 0-6-0PT No 9704 works a local freight.

RIGHT: Smartly turned out, the Southall shed breakdown train awaits its next turn of duty, on 8 March 1958. Class 5700 0-6-0PT No 7730 was fitted with a lowered cab, and was built by the North British Locomotive Co in December 1929. It was withdrawn a year after the photograph was taken.

A picture full of interest taken on 2 May 1961. Churchward 'Small Prairie' '4575' class 2-6-2T No 5541 stands under the Brunel train shed at Tavistock South. The broad gauge dimensions allowed for three standard gauge tracks to be built. The '45XXs' were the mainstay of many West Country branch lines, the service here being Launceston to Plymouth. Tavistock boasted two stations: North, of the former London & South Western Railway, closed in 1968, and South, of the Great Western, closed in 1962. No 5541 is preserved on the Dean Forest Railway.

LEFT: Class 4575 2-6-2T No 5572, still in BR black, stands in the pleasant surroundings of Fowey station on the service from Lostwithiel to St Blazey, on 23 September 1960. The branch opened in 1869 and was closed to passengers in 1968, but china clay traffic continues, from Lostwithiel to Carne Point. No 5572 was withdrawn in September 1962, and fortunately, it is one of a number of the class to have survived into preservation and is based at the Didcot Railway Centre.

BELOW: Standing in the yard at Laira shed, Plymouth on 25 September 1960 is '4575' class 2-6-2T No 5531. The first 19 of the earlier '4500' class were built at Wolverhampton Works between 1906 and 1908, and were the last engines to be completed there. The '4575s' were all built at Swindon, with sloping-topped water tanks that were larger than those of the '4500s', entering traffic in June 1928. No 5531 was one of the last of the class to be withdrawn, in December 1964.

Small Prairie' No 5572 again, awaits the right away from Marsh Mills on a 'motor train' for Tavistock, on 29 August 1961. This station scene had changed little over the years. Situated east of Plymouth near Tavistock Junction, it was opened in 1861 and closed to all traffic in 1962. Today, this is the site of the Plym Valley Railway.

The last of the '4500' class 2-6-2Ts to be built, No 4574 approaches Liskeard with the branch train from Looe on 9 July 1961. Dick obviously took the photograph slightly early, to avoid the lamp pole from appearing to grow out of the loco and to position the Great Western Railway cast-iron sign. The branch opened in 1860 and is one of the few West Country lines to survive into the 21st century.

LEFT: A wonderful view from the train as it crosses Moorswater Viaduct on the main line from Plymouth, on 9 July 1960. The locomotive shed and water tank can be seen in the centre of the picture with a row of china clay wagons on the left of the shed. A pair of derelict lime kilns can be seen on the right by some sheds.

BOTTOM LEFT: Moving along to the shed we see '4500' class 2-6-2T No 4552 waiting with a ball clay train before continuing down the branch to Looe to collect additional traffic. Moorswater shed was originally built about 1861 to serve as the locomotive and carriage workshops for the Liskeard & Looe and Liskeard & Caradon railways, which made an end-on junction at this point. The GWR took over the workings of both companies in 1909.

BELOW LEFT: No visit to Moorswater shed was complete without going to the 'gents', which was the firebox wrapper from 0-6-0ST *Caradon*, the L&CR's first new locomotive, which was located over the fast-flowing East Looe River.

No 4410 was one of the small class of '4400' 2-6-2Ts built for light and steeply
graded branches and is seen at Yelverton on 5 July 1955, awaiting departure time
on the service to Princetown. The signalbox to the left of the picture is situated
on the platform on the line to Tavistock.

Ingra Tor Halt on the Princetown branch with '4400' Class 2-6-2T No 4410 in the distance. The halt was opened in 1936, as something of an afterthought as the branch opened in 1883. As can be seen from the photograph from 5 July 1955, it was rather a bleak location, even in the summer. Princetown was the highest station in England at 1,373 feet above sea level; the line had a ruling gradient of 1 in 40. It was closed to all traffic on 5 March 1956.

No 4410 is seen again later the same day as it runs into Dousland station on the service to Princetown. The branch wound its way from Yelverton to Princetown, high up on Dartmoor serving some tiny villages and hamlets in this remote and desolate area. Thankfully, Dick was able to record the branch on the last summer of operation in 1956. No 4410 was withdrawn two months after this photograph was taken.

ABOVE: Class 5700 0-6-0PT No 3686, built at Swindon in 1940, approaches Marsh Mills with a freight from Tavistock on 30 August 1961. The engine served until July 1965 when it was withdrawn from traffic.

RIGHT: No 3787, a '5700' class 0-6-0PT, shunts stock at Chard Junction on 15 June 1962. The GWR line to Chard and Taunton can be seen curving away to the right, this closing that year. This was the junction with the LSWR main line to Exeter, and although the line to the west remains open, the station closed in 1966

Class 6400 0-6-0PT No 6430 stands at Seaton Junction on the branch train from Seaton. This class of 40 locomotives was similar to the '5400s' but were fitted for auto-working and had slightly larger driving wheels. No 6430 was built at Swindon Works in March 1937 and was withdrawn October 1964 having served its final years on the ex-London & South Western branch lines, as seen here in July 1963. Acquired as a source of spare parts following withdrawal, it has only recently been restored to working order, on the Llangollen Railway.

C. B. Collett designed the very useful 0-4-2T locomotives for use on Great Western branch lines, mainly for auto working. No 1471 is seen here at Bampton on the 10.26am Exeter to Dulverton service on 2 July 1963. This rural scene has completely disappeared, the line closing a few months after the photograph was taken and the station demolished and the cutting filled in.

ABOVE: Class 1400 0-4-2T, No 1445, stands at Sharpness on 16 July 1964, a few months before the line shut. The LMS station sign is a give-away as the branch from Berkeley Road was Midland/GW Joint, then LMS/GW Joint. No 1445 was withdrawn from service in September 1964.

LEFT: Class 1400 0-4-2T No 1467 at Yeovil Town station on the auto-train shuttle to Yeovil Junction on 10 July 1956. Yeovil had three stations: Town, shown here, closed in 1961; Pen Mill on the line from Castle Cary to Dorchester, which remains open, as does Yeovil Junction on the South Western main line to Exeter.

ABOVE: Former Cardiff Railway 0-4-0ST No 1338 stands at Bridgwater Docks on 7 July 1959. The locomotive was built by Kitson (No 3799 of 1898) for the Cardiff Railway which was absorbed into the GWR in 1923, and it passed into British Railways ownership, being the last ex-CR locomotive to survive. It was withdrawn in September 1963 and purchased for preservation in April 1964, and is now at the Didcot Railway Centre. The dock lines had a speed restriction of 5mph due to the crossing of six public roads and the engine was only allowed to operate in daylight and clear weather.

RIGHT: Class 1361 No 1363, one of Churchward's 0-6-0STs designed for dock shunting, was built at Swindon Works in 1910. Seen standing in Laira shed yard on 30 April 1961, it was used on shunting duties within the depot and in the Plymouth area. No 1363 was withdrawn in 1962 and is now preserved by the Great Western Society at Didcot.

A panoramic view of Exeter St Davids, showing the station on the extreme right, next to the very busy parcels depot. The engine shed with the coaling facility is on the left, and the yard with the four-road shed building is right. A 'Warship' class diesel-hydraulic stands in front of the 'factory'. The locomotives visible include 'Halls', '5101' class 2-6-2Ts and the inevitable pannier tanks. This scene has changed considerably since Dick took this photograph on 23 September 1962.

Dick was able to photograph the shed at Truro from the road, which passes the station, and not from the top of a signal gantry as he had done elsewhere! Locomotives in view include 'Manor' and 'Hall' class 4-6-0s, a '9400' class 0-6-0PT, and the roof of a 'Small Prairie'. The age of the diesel multiple unit had just begun and the front end of a new train can be seen outside the extended engine shed when this view was taken, on 22 July 1960.

Former Great Western diesel railcar No W12W heads west along the mainline in Sonning Cutting on 17 September 1955. The very successful fleet of 38 AEC-engined vehicles entered traffic from 1934. The first four of the class were bodied by Park Royal Coachworks, while those numbered from 5 to 18 were constructed by the Gloucester Carriage & Wagon Company. The remaining 20 were built at Swindon Works, between 1940 and 1942.

A fine view of Truro with the cathedral on the right of the photograph and by chance, there is a new diesel multiple unit in the siding. On a driver training run, the Birmingham Railway Carriage & Wagon Company-built unit (later to be Class 118) Nos W51317, W55449 and W51302, was only a few weeks old when this photograph was taken on 8 April 1960. The newly arrived units were based at Laira depot, Plymouth.

In the 1950s and '60s, holidays in camping coaches, located at various stations over the system, were popular. When most families travelled by train for their summer break it was very convenient to arrive at the station and within a few yards was the home for the holiday. Seen at Luxulyan on the branch from Par to Newquay, camping coach No W9906W stands in the station yard. The station boasted an island platform with pagoda-style waiting room, signalbox and water tower, but unfortunately, all this was swept away in 1964. The station remains open today as an unstaffed halt.

RIGHT: On withdrawal in May 1960, 'Castle' class 4-6-0 No 4073 *Caerphilly Castle* was stored for seven months at Swindon Works before being restored and moved to the Science Museum in London. The locomotive was moved from Park Royal to South Kensington by road. Seen en route in Du Cane Road, Hammersmith on 4 June 1961, the Pickfords' tractor and trailer is passed by London Transport bus No RTL 1400 on route 72 to Tolworth. Dick covered the event very well, taking more than 50 colour transparencies and an unknown quantity of black and white photographs!

Dick's view of a different photograph: 'Right away'. The guard of the 5.20pm Bristol Temple Meads to Severn Beach train, hauled by '6100' class 2-6-2T No 6107, waves his green flag as the train departs from Patchway on 20 September 1955.

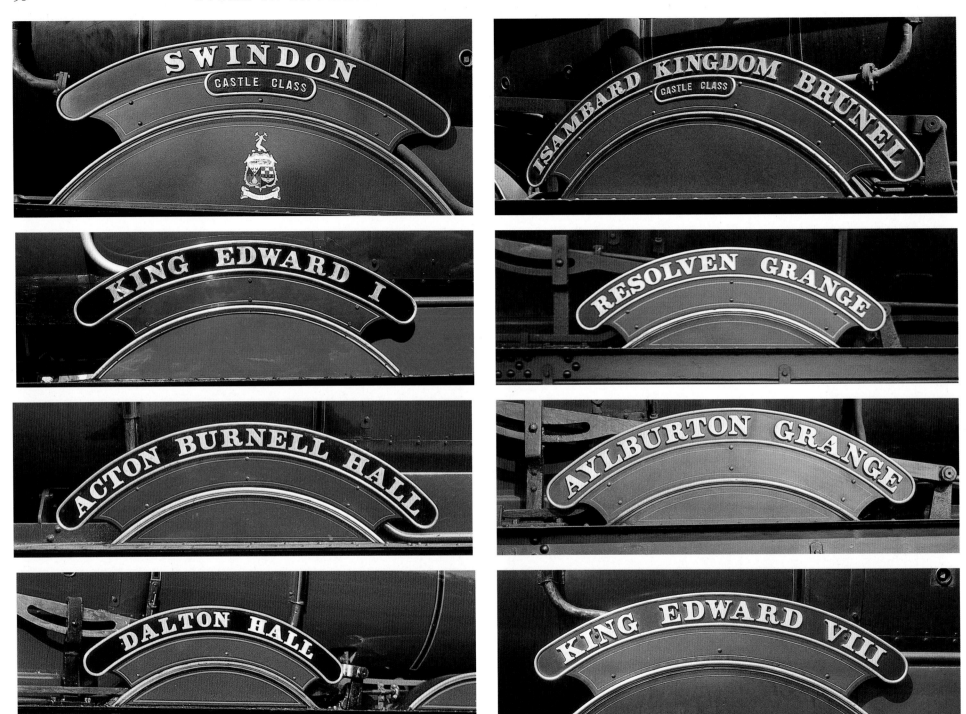

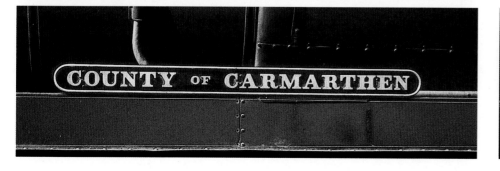

The Somerset & Dorset

Former Somerset & Dorset Joint Railway Class 7F 2-8-0 No 53807 leaves Wellow with a freight bound for Bath, having been shunted back into the sidings to allow the northbound 'Pines Express' to pass on 6 July 1959. The 11 2-8-0s spent all their lives on the S&D. The first batch, SDJR Nos 80–85 (BR Nos 53800–5), were built by the Midland Railway at Derby Works in 1914, specially for the S&D, while the second batch, with larger boilers, was built by Robert Stephenson & Co in 1925, SDJR Nos 86–90 (BR Nos 53806–10). No 53807 was the last of the '7Fs' to be withdrawn on 6 September 1964, the class having given 50 years of outstanding service. Fortunately, two of these fine locomotives have survived into preservation: Nos 53808 (88) on the West Somerset Railway, and 53809 at the Midland Railway — Butterley.

There is no doubting the identity of this train! BR Class 5MT 4-6-0 No 73087 *Linette* takes water while the assistant engine, Class 2P 4-4-0 No 40652, is uncoupled ready to return to Templecombe shed, having helped the train engine over the Mendip hills. The scene is Evercreech Junction on 6 July 1959, the ever-observant Dick Riley noted that the water tower in the distance carried a cast iron plate reading 'S&DR Wimbledon Ironworks 1892'. The 'Pines Express' ran every day apart from Sundays, connecting Liverpool and Manchester with Bournemouth. In the summer months, when many holidaymakers travelled by train, it proved to be a very popular service and often ran in duplicate.

LEFT: Class 2P 4-4-0 No 40563 pilots rebuilt 'West Country' Pacific 4-6-2 No 34028 *Eddystone* (now preserved on the Swanage Railway) as they burst out of Chilcompton Tunnel on the 6.52am Cleethorpes to Bournemouth West, on 5 September 1959. Dick spent many hours with his great friend Ivo Peters on the much-loved Somerset & Dorset, a line that ran through wonderful countryside, with beautifully kept stations. Ivo wrote in one of his many books on the S&D: 'To all my Somerset & Dorset friends, whose kindness and co-operation always made photography on the S&D such a very happy affair.' I am certain that Dick and many other photographers who visited the line would have echoed that statement!

RIGHT: With plenty of steam, Class 4F 0-6-0 No 44523 assists SDJR Class 7F 2-8-0 No 53801 entering the double line section at Midford with the 9.08am Birmingham to Bournemouth West, on 5 September 1959. The very tall lower quadrant signal was a distinctive feature of this location. The choice of slide was not easy as a number were taken of this train as it travelled south; I think this was achieved with Ivo Peter's local knowledge and the aid of his Bentley!

Class 2P 4-4-0 No 40700 pilots BR Standard Class 5MT 4-6-0 No 73051 on the 9.55am Bournemouth West to Leeds, approaching Midford on 5 September 1959. The '2P' would have been attached at Evercreech Junction to provide assistance over the Mendip hills to Bath. The double track reduced to a single line by Midford station.

Class 3F 0-6-0 No 43218 (SDJR No 73) runs light engine at Cole, having just worked the 4.19pm milk train from Highbridge on 18 July 1959. The milk came from a dairy at Bason Bridge and was destined for the London market.

The locomotive was built by Neilson Reid & Co in 1902 and spent much of its life working the branch line from Evercreech Junction to Burnham-on-Sea.

A Mecca for photographers visiting the S&D – Templecombe shed. BR Class 5MT 4-6-0 No 73052 heads the 4.16pm stopping train from Evercreech Junction to Bournemouth West on 7 July 1959. The tall building in the centre of the photograph was used as the motive power offices and was the former Dorset Central Railway station. Class 2P 4-4-0 No 40634 (SDJR No 45) and a '4F' 0-6-0 stand by the main line and in the background can be seen a BR Standard and a '7F'. The turntable at the shed was too short to turn the 2-8-0s!

On the southern section of the S&D, Shillingstone station was opened in 1863, the photograph showing the small, 16-lever signalbox, based on a London & South Western Railway design, together with a friendly signalman. The staff on the S&D were always helpful and many of the signalmen were very happy to have a chat and to update the photographer on traffic movements. Note the wagons in the goods yard and the very ornate awning on the shed by the signalbox, and what must have been S&D fire buckets under the stairs. The station closed to freight in April 1965 and to passengers on 7 March 1966.

London Midland Region

'Princess Coronation' class 4-6-2 No 46226 *Duchess of Norfolk* stands at Carlisle waiting to head a southbound express from Glasgow on 27 May 1959. This class of 38 locomotives was designed by Sir William Stanier and introduced in 1938. All were built at Crewe Works between 1937 and 1948, with building suspended in 1942 for the 'duration'. *Duchess of Norfolk* was withdrawn in October 1964. Fortunately, three of the class survived the cutter's torch: No 46229 *Duchess of Hamilton*, now in the National Collection and recently re-streamlined; No 46233 *Duchess of Sutherland*, preserved by the Princess Royal Locomotive Trust at Butterley and currently operational on the main line; and No 46235 *City of Birmingham*, in the Birmingham Science Museum.

'Royal Scot' class 4-6-0 No 46100 *Royal Scot* at Derby shed on 25 May 1955, built as No 6152 *The King's Dragoon Guardsman*, but exchanging identity permanently with No 6100 in January 1933 for a visit to the USA. The 71 locomotives of this class were introduced in 1927 by Sir Henry Fowler. Numbers 6100–6149 were built by the North British Locomotive Co at Glasgow, and Nos 6150–6169 constructed at Derby Works, while No 6170 was a notional rebuild of No 6399 *Fury*. This was the prelude to Stanier rebuilding the 'Royal Scots' and 'Patriots'. Two 'Royal Scots' survived into preservation, *Royal Scot* and No 46115 *Scots Guardsman*, both now active on the main line.

A fine late-evening shot of 'Patriot' class 4-6-0 No 45511 *Isle of Man* as it simmers at Willesden shed on 29 August 1959. This locomotive was built at Crewe in 1932 but was not named until 1938. The crest of the island above the nameplate is clearly visible. The class was introduced in 1930 by Sir Henry Fowler, the first two locomotives being rebuilds of London & North Western Railway 'Claughton' class 4-6-0s, but the remaining 50 locomotives were built new, from 1933. Unfortunately, none of the class survived into preservation, although a project to build a new example has recently been launched.

'Princes Royal' class 4-6-2 No 46207 *Princess Arthur of Connaught* climbs Camden Bank with a Euston to Liverpool express on 20 September 1958. This class was designed by Sir William Stanier and introduced in 1933, being the most powerful passenger locomotive on the LMS at that time. The 12 locomotives were built at Crewe, in addition to which was No 6202, built as the turbine-driven Turbomotive. It was rebuilt at Crewe as a conventional piston-driven locomotive in 1952, but as No 46202 *Princess Anne* it was the train engine of the 8.30am Euston to Liverpool express which was one of the trains involved in the Harrow & Wealdstone accident on 8 October 1952. The locomotive was damaged beyond repair. Fortunately *Princess Elizabeth* and *Princess Margaret Rose* have been preserved.

The first 60 of the '3F' class 0-6-0Ts were introduced by Johnson from 1899 for the Midland Railway, and from 1924, the LMS produced a further 417 locomotives as a development of the original design. No 47529 is seen here at Camden shed on 16 February 1958, just over three years before withdrawal. The original Camden roundhouse can be seen in the background, which survives today as a performing arts venue.

The '3MT' class 2-6-2T mixed-traffic locomotives were introduced in 1930 to a Fowler design. All were built at Derby between March 1930 and November 1933 and of the total build of 70 engines, 20 were fitted with condensing apparatus for working on London Transport lines to Moorgate. No 40049 is seen stored at Willesden shed on 13 March 1961. The class had become extinct by December 1962.

In 1946, H. G. Ivatt introduced the mixed-traffic '2MT' class 2-6-0s for general work. In total, 128 locomotives were built between 1946 and 1953: 65 at Crewe, 38 at Darlington, and 25 at Swindon. A very clean No 46424 moves slowly past the coaling plant at Willesden shed on 18 March 1961.

The LMS had a very large variety of '4MT' class 2-6-4Ts, introduced by Fowler, Stanier and Fairburn. Between 1927 and 1945, 645 locomotives were built: 125 to the design of Fowler, 392 Stanier and 128 Fairburn. No 42422, seen here at Willesden shed on 2 April 1960, was one of the Fowler engines and was fitted with a side-window cab. It was withdrawn in December 1962.

Johnson introduced the '2F' class 0-6-0s for the Midland Railway in 1876. Most were rebuilt with Belpaire boilers from 1917 and many of the class were withdrawn long ago, but a small number of the class survived into BR days. These were based on Coalville shed for working the goods service on the West Bridge, Leicester to Desford Junction branch. No 58148 is seen leaving the narrow-bore, 1,796 yd Glenfield Tunnel on 2 May 1963. The branch formed part of the Leicester & Swannington Railway which was one of the earliest steam-operated lines in England. Opened to passengers on 27 April 1833, it closed to such traffic on 24 September 1928, while goods services lasted until 29 April 1962.

RIGHT: A post-Grouping development of the Johnson Midland Compound '4P' class 4-4-0 was introduced in 1924, with 195 engines constructed, of which no fewer than 190 were built in the short space of 3½ years between then and 1927. The building of the locomotives was shared between Derby and Horwich works of the LMS, the North British Locomotive Co, and Vulcan Foundry. No 41090 makes a sad sight as it awaits its fate at Derby on 24 May 1959 following withdrawal from service in December 1958. One of the class, MR No 1000, survives as part of the National Collection.

RIGHT: Locomotives seen awaiting the cutter's torch, stored on the Burton line siding, Derby, on 24 May, had become a familiar sight in 1959. Dick's records show that the line of condemned engines included Nos 40553, 47249, 58157, 58192, 40420, 41083, 43186, 41122, 41113, 58215 and 43300.

FAR RIGHT: Preserved Midland Compound 4-4-0 No 1000 enters Derby with the Stephenson Locomotive Society 'Golden Jubilee Special' on 27 September 1959. The tour ran from Birmingham New Street to Derby, Toton and Nottingham Midland for works and shed visits; the cost of the tour was 10s 6d (52½p)!

C. J. Bowen-Cooke of the London & North Western Railway introduced the 'G2a' class '7F' 0-8-0 heavy goods engines in 1921. More than 300 examples of Classes G1, G2 and G2a were built between 1912 and 1936. No 49287 ambles into Oxford with a northbound freight on 29 September 1956. It was withdrawn from Bletchley shed on November 1962. It is interesting to note that the wooden wagon behind the engine still carries private-owner lettering.

Sir William Stanier further developed the 'Patriot' Class with the introduction of a taper-boiler 4-6-0 class known as the 'Jubilees'. Introduced in 1934, a total of 190 locomotives were built at Crewe and by the North British Locomotive Co at its Queen's Park and Hyde Park works in Glasgow. No 45734 *Meteor* leaves Wolverhampton High level with the 11.50am to Euston on 19 October 1959. *Meteor* was withdrawn on 28 December 1963 and cut up at Crewe Works the following year, having served for only 27 years, in which time it was based at seven different depots.

British Railways Standard Class 4 4-6-0 No 75046, built at Swindon Works in 1952 and allocated to the London Midland Region, heads a train of four coaches over Walkden troughs on a local service from Manchester to Bolton on 12 April 1959. At the time, the locomotive was allocated to Bank Hall depot; it was withdrawn from Stoke-on-Trent depot in August 1967, being cut up by Birds Commercial Motors, Long Marston, in February 1968. Six members of the class have been preserved.

A total of 580 locomotives built to a Fowler design were introduced in 1924 as a post-Grouping development of the Midland Railway's Class 4F 0-6-0. One of these, No 44420, is seen at Bixley Sidings, Burton-on-Trent, on 26 May 1959 – did the crew receive a print, I wonder?

Fowler-designed Class 3MT 2-6-2T No 40053 climbs Camden Bank out of Euston on empty stock working on 3 October 1959. Built at Derby in September 1931, No 40053 was withdrawn from service in August 1961.

The most numerous class on the LMSR, the maids of all work were the Stanier Class 5MT 4-6-0s, no fewer than 842 locomotives being built between 1934 and 1947. Vulcan Foundry at Newton-le-Willows built 100, Armstrong Whitworth 327, Horwich Works 120, Derby Works 54, and Crewe Works 241. No 45426 is seen leaving Kensington Olympia on the summer Saturday Hastings to Manchester working. This is a picture full of interest, showing the long-since-removed signals and signalbox, and a train of very mixed stock, on 22 August 1959.

ABOVE: Dick spent a very successful day at Staveley, Derbyshire, on 5 March 1961. Ex-Midland Railway Class 1F 0-6-0T No 41734 shunts the Staveley Iron & Chemical Co's works, this being one of a class of 137 engines built to S. W. Johnson's design, between 1878 and 1892. There was an agreement between the iron company and the Midland Railway for the supply of locomotives to shunt the works sidings for 100 years. One of the Staveley 0-6-0Ts, No 41708, has been preserved.

RIGHT: Former Lancashire & Yorkshire Railway Aspinall dock tank Class 1F 0-6-0T No 51537 awaits its next call of duty at Liverpool docks. This photograph was taken at Bankfield Goods, near the Alexandra and Canada Dock, on 11 April 1959. This engine was the last survivor of 20 LYR Class 24s built at Horwich in 1897, was withdrawn from Aintree shed in September 1961. Note the wonderful chimney lid which was fitted to deflect sparks and smoke from rising into the girders of the Liverpool Overhead Railway which ran above the dock lines in places.

RIGHT: Another Class 1F 0-6-0T, No 41739, is different from No 41734 in that it is fitted with a half-cab. It shunts a rake of 16-ton steel mineral-wagons. Obviously the visit was arranged by an enthusiast group who were allowed access to the site before the days of high-visibility clothing!

BELOW: Midland Railway Deeley design Class 0F 0-4-0T No 41533, introduced in 1907, moves off to its next turn of duty within works at Staveley. The locomotive was built at Derby in 1921 and withdrawn in December 1966.

ABOVE: Activity in Bristol LMS shed yard as Fowler Class 4F 0-6-0 No 44092 draws out Aspinall-designed Class 0F 0-4-0ST No 51218. The depot had two Lancashire & Yorkshire Railway 'Pugs' which were used for shunting the restricted Avonside Wharf branch. Bristol had three main locomotive depots, with Barrow Road, the site of this photograph, the last to close to steam, in October 1965.

RIGHT: It might be a diesel multiple unit, but who could resist this very interesting view at Derby on 24 May 1959? Unfortunately, Dick did not record the number of this new unit as it passed the south end of the station.

Stanier Class 8F 2-8-0 No 48194 leaves Clifford Sidings near Stratford-on-Avon (Old Town) on the Stratford & Midland Junction Railway, heading a freight bound for Bedford on 24 May 1957. The '8Fs' were the mainstay of the freight workings of the LMS, being introduced by Stanier in 1935, with 852 of the class built and 666 later being taken into BR stock. Judging by the planting in the foreground, the signalman must have had plenty of time to tend his plants!

Locomotives in Industry

A Mackenzie & Holland ground signal at Port of London Authority, Custom House on 25 September 1957.

The Port of London Authority locomotive shed at Custom House on 14 September 1957. The locomotives in view are PLA No 90, 0-6-0T (Hudswell Clarke 1873 of 1954), PLA No 79, 0-6-0ST (Hunslet 2414 of 1941 – supplied to the War Department, their No 70066, loaned to PLA in 1943, and purchased in May 1946), and PLA No 45, 0-6-0T (Hudswell Clarke 1101 of 1915). No 45 was withdrawn in 1959 and scrapped on site by George Cohen & Sons by November 1959 while No 90 went to Cox & Danks for scrap in April 1963. No 79 was sold to the NCB and used at Ackton Hall Colliery, West Yorkshire in October 1960, ending its life in industry at Snydale Colliery, it was then sold to the Yorkshire Dales Railway in June 1976 and is there today on what is now the Embsay & Bolton Abbey Steam Railway.

North Thames Gas Board, Beckton, East London, which was one of the largest gas works in the world with an internal railway system to match. During the period 1869–1970 as many as 84 different locomotives were used. The fleet was unique in that all the locomotives were cut down to enable access to restricted retort houses. With such a wonderful selection of locomotives it is understandable that Dick made many visits over the years. No 1, 0-4-0WT (Neilson 1561 of 1870; rebuilt at Beckton in 1929) and No 25, 0-4-0ST (Neilson 5087 of 1896) stand outside the roundhouse on 24 August 1957. Both locomotives have been preserved: No 1 can be seen at the Penrhyn Castle Industrial Railway Museum near Bangor in North Wales, and No 25 is at Bressingham Steam Museum, Norfolk. The site at Beckton was used as a location for a number of film sets including the opening sequence of the 1981 James Bond movie *For Your Eyes Only*.

Beckton By-Products Works No 13, 0-4-0ST (Hawthorn Leslie 3308 of 1918) poses in the sunshine on 23 November 1961. This locomotive was scrapped at Beckton in July 1967.

86

John Mowlem & Co Ltd, Marshmoor Works, Welham Green near Hatfield, where 0-6-0ST *London John* (Hudswell Clarke 1593 of 1927) stands in the yard on 30 April 1960. The site was situated on the west of the BR East Coast main line, two miles south of Hatfield station and was used to store the company's extensive railway stock. *London John* worked on various sites over the years and was scrapped in April 1965.

The Ford Motor Co works at Dagenham has an extensive railway network and at one time had a fleet of steam locomotives. In beautiful condition, 0-6-0ST Ford No 7 (Peckett 1938 of 1937) awaits the next turn of duty on 16 May 1961. Christine's father and elder sister both worked at the Dagenham factory, but it is not known whether they had any interest in the railway system! No 7 was sold and scrapped in 1967.

ECC Ports (a division of English China Clays Ltd), Par Harbour. The area had an extensive rail network to serve the various quays, mainly used for the export of china clay. At one point the line ran beneath the Great Western main line through a low tunnel, which necessitated the locomotives being specially designed. Here we see *Judy*, an 0-4-0ST (Bagnall 2572 of 1937), resting between duties on 24 July 1960. This locomotive moved to St Austell China Clay Museum for preservation in June 1978 but later moved to the Bodmin & Wenford Railway to join *Alfred* (Bagnall 3058 of 1953) the other cut-down loco from Par, both of which are now back in working order, for the first time for 30 years.

Cadbury's, Bournville. Cadbury No 1, 0-4-0T (Avonside 1977 of 1925) stands in the yard at Bournville on 4 March 1961. This locomotive fitted with outside Walschaerts valve gear was saved for preservation, being moved to the Dowty Railway Preservation Society, Ashchurch in February 1963. It worked the first trains on the Gloucestershire Warwickshire Railway and is now preserved at Tyseley.

RIGHT: Park Gate Iron & Steel Co Ltd, Charwelton Quarries in Northamptonshire. The quarries were situated off the GCR main line near Charwelton station. Here, we see 0-4-0ST No 8 (Yorkshire 784 of 1905), with its running number carried on the front of the chimney. This locomotive was moved from Park Gate Ironworks in February 1952 and was scrapped in November 1963, two years after the quarry had closed in November 1961.

ABOVE RIGHT: Staveley Coal & Iron Co Ltd, Derbyshire, 0-4-0ST *Peterstone* (Manning Wardle 1023 of 1887). Delivered new to T. A. Walker, St Fagans, Glamorgan, rebuilt by the builder in 1907 then to Staveley where it spent the rest of its working life. Dick photographed it on 5 March 1961, just prior to scrapping by Steel Breaking & Dismantling, Chesterfield.

RIGHT: Staveley Coal & Iron Co Ltd. Staveley shed was host to three Markham-constructed 0-4-0ST locomotives: *G. Bond* (107 of 1893), *Gladys* (109 of 1894) and *Staveley* (105 of 1891); this view date is 5 March 1961. *G. Bond* and *Staveley* were both scrapped on site in 1965, but *Gladys* survived the cutter's torch and is now at the Midland Railway — Butterley.

RIGHT: NCB Walsall Wood Colliery, Staffordshire. No 5 *Lord Kitchener,* 0-6-0ST (Kitson 5158 of 1915) was delivered new to the colliery where the first shaft was sunk in 1874. A small fleet of locomotives was used to shunt the various sidings on the LNWR branch between Aldridge and Brownhills. No 5 spent its life at the colliery apart from visits to Cannock Chase Central Workshops for repair. The photograph was taken on 1 May 1963, two years before the loco was scrapped.

LEFT: Leicester Gas Works. Coal gas was first produced by the Leicester Gas Company as early as 1821 and the chemical works was opened in 1886 with the rail system completed at that time. The first locomotive had appeared on the site in 1885. Over the years, the system was expanded and two locomotives were normally used, one to shunt the sidings alongside the Leicester to Burton branch while the other performed duties within works. The locomotive fleet was maintained on site where all repairs and overhauls were carried out. The locomotives were very well maintained; here we see 0-4-0ST *Mars II,* (Robert Stephenson & Hawthorns (Newcastle) 7493), new to Leicester in 1948. Gas production ceased in May 1969, the rail system having closed the year before. Fortunately, *Mars II* was saved from scrap and is now at the Snibston Discovery Park at Coalville.

British Sugar Corporation, Wissington, A very extensive railway known at the Wissington Light Railway ran through many miles of bleak Fenland country to serve the local agriculture near Stoke Ferry in Norfolk. The railway opened in 1905 and by 1925 the railway attained 20 miles and in the same year the sugar factory was built at Wissington. The railway had a fleet of locomotives serving the factory, moving agricultural produce, coal and sugar beet. Sadly, rail traffic ceased at the end of 1981 much to the regret of many photographers. Dick visited the site on a number of occasions with his friend Dr Ian C. Allen. Here we see 0-6-0ST *Wissington* (Hudswell Clarke 1700 of 1938) shunting within the factory on 17 December 1967. This locomotive is now preserved in Norfolk and is currently stripped down for restoration.

LEFT: Bass, Ratcliffe & Gretton, Burton-on-Trent. A very extensive railway network built after several acts of Parliament, between 1860 and 1880. The Acts enabled the construction of connecting branch lines and sidings throughout the town of Burton linking many of the breweries with the main line. The Bass private railway first came into use in 1862. Here we see 0-4-0ST No 9 (Neilson Reid 5907 of 1901) shunting wagons alongside the Middle Brewery and hop store on 12 April 1958. This locomotive hauled a saloon for King Edward VIII on 22 May 1902 when he inspected the area. The locomotive and saloon are now preserved in the former Bass Museum, which unfortunately, under the ownership of Coors, closed during 2008, although to date they remain on site.

LEFT: Worthington & Co Ltd, Burton-on-Trent. Worthington 0-4-0ST No 2 (Hudswell Clarke 690 of 1904) emerges on to the Hay branch from the Worthington premises, 29 September 1957. The locomotive was delivered new to Worthington in January 1904 and spent its working life in the area, becoming part of the Bass fleet in May 1960. It was allocated the number 14, but this was never carried. The locomotive was removed to Derby and scrapped in June 1961.

BELOW: Bowaters United Kingdom Pulp & Paper Mills Ltd, Sittingbourne, Kent. The 2ft 6in gauge line here was the very last steam-operated industrial narrow gauge railway in the United Kingdom. Fortunately, when the line closed in October 1969 the Locomotive Club of Great Britain took on a lease to preserve and continue to run the railway between Kemsley Down and Sittingbourne, although it is not operational at the time of writing. The line ran from Ridham Dock to Kemsley and on to Sittingbourne and was used to move pulp bales from the dock to the works as well as a passenger service for the workers. *Excelsior*, 0-4-2ST (Kerr Stuart 1049 of 1908) stands at Ridham Dock on 14 May 1960. This locomotive can now be seen working at Whipsnade Wild Animal Park in Bedfordshire, but the main fleet of the original locomotives remain at the SKLR.

British Portland Cement Manufacturers Ltd, Wouldham Works, West Thurrock. A wonderful working scene at the Essex site that is now covered by the Lakeside shopping centre. 0-4-0ST *Arab,* (Peckett 800 of 1899) seen at work with some old tippler wagons on 23 March 1957, was scrapped on site in July 1961.

National Coal Board, Betteshanger Colliery, near Deal, Kent – the last outpost of steam east of the Medway. In this May 1959 view we see a busy yard with two 0-6-0STs in action: *St Martin* (Avonside 2064 of 1931) and No 9 (Hunslet 3825 of 1954) which is surprisingly clean. *St Martin* moved to Snowdown Colliery in June 1966 and was scrapped in December 1973. No 9 also moved to Snowdown in December 1972 and then on to the Main Line Steam Trust, Loughborough for preservation in November 1981, and is now at Carnforth.

Eastern Region

LNER Gresley Class V2 2-6-2 No 60800 *Green Arrow* was built at Doncaster in 1936, works number 1837. Originally numbered 4771 and renumbered 800 by the LNER in November 1946, it then became BR No 60800 in February 1949. After serving 26 years, almost entirely spent based at King's Cross shed, it was withdrawn on 21 August 1962. It was restored at Doncaster, including the fitting of a replacement boiler and repainted in LNER apple green with its original number, 4771. However, with no space available at the new Museum of British Transport at Clapham it was to spend many years in store. A change of policy regarding steam on the national network resulted in it being fully restored to running condition in 1972/3, returning to the main line in June 1973. Since then, many main line miles have been covered before final withdrawal in 2008. The photograph was taken at Top shed on 16 September 1961.

RIGHT: What must have been Gresley's finest design, the 'A4' class Pacific. Here we see No 60017 *Silver Fox* at King's Cross shed on 18 March 1961. A total of 35 'A4s' was built between 1935 and 1938. In Dick Riley's notes he reported a visit to this shed, and I quote his words: 'It was in April 1936 that I first joined a party to visit Top shed. By this time all four silver 'A4s' were in service, Nos 2509/10 at King's Cross to be joined by Nos 2512 *Silver Fox*, with 2511 *Silver King* being at Gateshead.' The young Riley was just 15 at the time of his visit! There must have been very many visits over the subsequent years so this shot of *Silver Fox* in 1961 must have been very special to him.

RIGHT: LNER Gresley Class A3 Pacific No 60055 *Woolwinder* at King's Cross on 18 March 1961. The locomotive was built at Doncaster Works in 1924, it carried the works number 1610 and was rebuilt from 'A1' to 'A3' in June 1942, receiving a double chimney in June 1958. It was withdrawn from service in September 1961, having run over 2,000,000 miles.

LEFT: An amazing picture: this view of Moorgate was obtained on 30 July 1958 by climbing on to scaffolding and taking the picture over a high wall during the re-development of a local property. It is not known whether permission was obtained! 'N2' class 0-6-2T No 69523 (now preserved on the Great Central Railway) departs with the 5.20pm to Welwyn Garden City while an ex-LMS Fowler Class 3P 2-6-2T awaits its next turn of duty. The brown livery of the London Transport 'T Stock' behind the 'N2' is of interest, all of which had disappeared by October 1962.

ABOVE: Beautifully prepared Class J69 0-6-0T No 68619 and Class N7 0-6-2T No 69614 spent most of their time in the shadows of Liverpool Street station, but to quote Dick: 'On a slack Saturday afternoon, 11 May 1957, I asked Ted Carron, Running Foreman at Liverpool Street if he would be kind enough to arrange for the locos to be turned to face into the sun. Rather to my surprise he agreed to do so, providing a unique photograph and giving the youthful observers on the taxicab road an unexpected treat.' No doubt Mr Carron was provided with suitable prints.

'Sandringham' Class B17/6 4-6-0 No 61652 *Darlington* leaves Cambridge with the Sunday, 9.50am stopping train to King's Cross. This locomotive was built at Darlington by the LNER in 1936, originally numbered 2852 and renumbered 1652 in 1946, becoming BR No 61652 in April 1949, and withdrawn from service in September 1959. In the background can be seen LMR Class 2MT 2-6-0 No 46466 about to work an excursion to Clacton via the Colne Valley line. The date is 22 June 1958.

Another 'Sandringham', No 61656 *Leeds United*, attacks Bethnal Green bank on 28 February 1959 with the 12.33pm Liverpool Street to Yarmouth South Town. *Leeds United* succumbed to the cutter's torch in 1960. Unfortunately, none of this handsome class survived into preservation, but the Sandringham Locomotive Company is currently building two examples from scratch.

Gresley Class K3 2-6-0 No 61834 takes water at the north end of Cambridge station on 16 June 1960. The Dick Riley caption from the Atlantic series *The Great Eastern Lines* is repeated in full: 'Richard Hardy, the DMPS at Stratford, knowing my taste for footplate riding enquired whether I had ever had a footplate ride on a K3. I had not done so and as they were rostered on the 4.36pm Liverpool Street–Bury St Edmunds this was arranged, and the late Len Theobald,

Chief Locomotive Inspector accompanied me. However, the Cambridge driver greeted me with the words: "You've come on the wrong night, Guv. We've got a ruddy K3 tonight." Could there be a better caption? The locomotive was built at Darlington in 1924 and numbered 120, renumbered 1834 in June 1946, to BR No 61834 in April 1948, and withdrawn in May 1962.

After Nationalisation, 70 locomotives of the 'K1' class were built between 1949 and 1950. No 62051, photographed on a freight train at Bishops Stortford on 12 September 1959, was built by the North British Locomotive Co (builder's No 26655) in November 1949, and after a short lifespan was withdrawn in January 1965.

A classic 4-4-0, No 62543, built at the Great Eastern Railway's Stratford Works in December 1903; reclassified from 'D15' to 'D16/2' in February 1928 and to 'D16/3' in February 1949, but sadly withdrawn in October 1958. Unfortunately, the final 'Claud Hamilton' was withdrawn in October 1960, never again to grace the East Anglian scene of which they were so much a part. No 62543 simmers in Cambridge shed yard on 19 May 1957.

We now see a locomotive that has survived into preservation. Class B12 No 61572, an inside-cylinder 4-6-0 built in 1928 by Beyer Peacock (builder's No 6488), stands outside Stratford shed on 7 May 1961, a few months before withdrawal. No 61572 outlasted the remainder of the class by nearly two years and became a favourite on many railtour duties and therefore became a contender for preservation. A visitor to the North Norfolk Railway will see this fine locomotive.

Edward Thompson of the LNER designed a handsome 4-6-0 locomotive classified 'B1', a total of 410 being built between 1942 and 1952. Seen here is immaculate No 61135 at Stratford shed on 10 August 1958, a contrast to another member of the class behind! No 61135 was built by the North British Locomotive Co (builder's No 25891) in March 1947. Survival was only 16 years, being withdrawn in 1963. This was a Parkeston engine for many years, regularly manned by Driver R. Fleming and Fireman R. Harvey – information from Dick Hardy's excellent memory!

Built by the GNR in 1918 as Class O4 No 6545, rebuilt as an 'O1' in May 1945, renumbered in November 1946 as 3650 and becoming BR No 63650 in September 1949, this 2-8-0 was withdrawn from service in June 1965. Seen at Stratford depot on 6 March 1958 having worked a train of coal from Whitemoor yard for Stratford's coaling plant.

A locomotive with a remarkable history. Built by the LNER in 1923, *Flying Scotsman* travelled over 2,000,000 miles in LNER and BR service and was withdrawn in January 1963. With great foresight, Mr Alan Pegler purchased No 60103 from British Railways and over the following years many special trains were run, hauled by this famous locomotive, restored as No 4472. When steam ceased on BR in 1968, it became the only steam locomotive permitted to run on the main line and this was only because its owner had a contract with BR extending to 1972. Here, No 4472 climbs Sapperton bank, towards Swindon – a foreigner on Great Western territory, on 16 August 1964. The locomotive is now part of the National Collection at York.

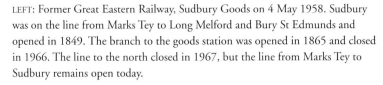

LEFT: Former Great Eastern Railway, Sudbury Goods on 4 May 1958. Sudbury was on the line from Marks Tey to Long Melford and Bury St Edmunds and opened in 1849. The branch to the goods station was opened in 1865 and closed in 1966. The line to the north closed in 1967, but the line from Marks Tey to Sudbury remains open today.

BELOW LEFT: Linton station, opened by the Great Eastern Railway in 1866, a year after the line opened in 1865, was situated on the line between Shelford and Bartlow which closed in 1967. A very peaceful scene on 27 April 1958, and from the original caption Dick notes the blue sign: 'You may telephone from here'.

BELOW: A wonderful signal gantry at Thames Wharf Junction, seen on 31 March 1962. The double bracket signal controlled the exit from Thames Wharf yard on the North Woolwich line. The design was by McKenzie & Holland, the original Great Eastern lower quadrant signals long since replaced by upper quadrants. In the middle distance the main line curving in from the right is from Custom House to Canning Town.

ABOVE: British Railways Standard 'Britannia' Class 4-6-2 No 70034 *Thomas Hardy* passes Bethnal Green on the 9.45am express from Norwich to Liverpool Street, 28 February 1959. The 'Britannia' Pacifics were the mainstay of the Great Eastern express services until replaced by BR Type 3 (now Class 37) and Type 4 (Class 40) diesel-electrics in 1961.

LEFT: Class L1 2-6-4T No 67767 departs from Wood Green on an empty stock working to King's Cross, to form a northbound rush hour train on 13 September 1958. This class was designed for the LNER by Thompson with No. 67767 built by Robert Stephenson & Hawthorns in 1949. All 100 were withdrawn by December 1962 after a very short working life, none survived the cutters torch.

Great Eastern Railway Class J15 No 65443 working a Railway Enthusiast Club special on the Kelvedon & Tollesbury Light Railway on 6 April 1957. The enthusiasts loaded in open wagons are seen near Inworth. The 9¾-mile branch was opened in 1904 and closed to passengers in May 1951, and to freight in September 1962.

For many years, the Cambridge University Railway Club had a tradition of running an 'Engine Driving and Firing Special' each spring, between Linton and Haverhill on the Stour Valley line. The last surviving Great Eastern Class E4 2-4-0, No 62785, is seen departing from Haverhill on 27 April 1958. How 'health and safety' would view such an exercise today is not known! This locomotive is now part of the National Collection and on display at Bressingham Steam Museum.

A small harbour on the River Alde existed before the Snape Maltings were built in the mid-1850s, at which time, the 1½-mile branch was built by the East Suffolk Railway, and opened in 1859. The branch left the main line at Snape Junction, three miles south of Saxmundham, it never had a passenger service and was used to serve the maltings. Class J15 No 65389 is seen crossing the timber trestle bridge over the River Alde on 3 May 1958.

Class N5 0-6-2T No 69262, a
former Manchester, Sheffield &
Lincolnshire Railway locomotive,
shunts the yard at Stamford East,
the end of a four-mile branch from
Essendine. The locomotive is
shunting the daily pick-up goods
from Peterborough on 25 June
1958. This class was designed by
T. Parker and 129 engines were
built between 1891 and 1901.
No 69262 emerged from Beyer
Peacock's works in 1893, and was
withdrawn in 1959.

The Saffron Walden branch, running from Audley End to Bartlow, was opened in 1865 by the independent Saffron Walden Railway. It was purchased by the Great Eastern Railway in 1877 and was closed to all traffic in 1964. Here we see Class G5 0-4-4T No 67322 at Bartlow; built at Darlington in 1900, it was withdrawn in November 1956, just three months after this photograph was taken.

Dick carefully noted an interesting fact that the second coach, No E63423E, was built in 1897 for the Cromer express services and converted for push-and-pull operation in 1939 for the Palace Gates line, moving to Saffron Walden in 1951. Where would we be without such gems of information?

Cast in Iron

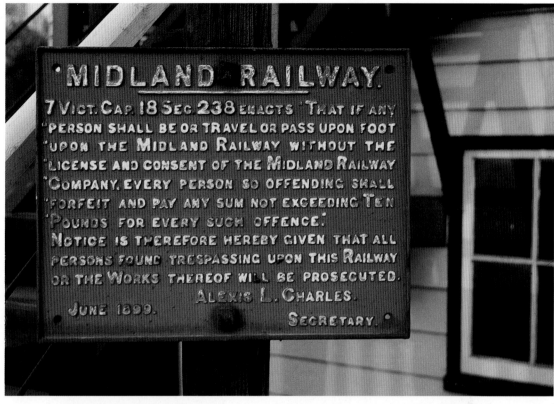

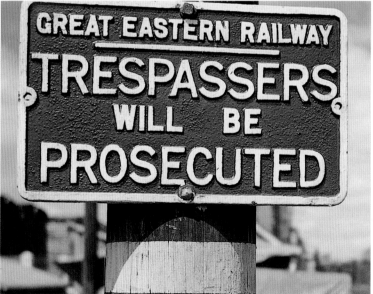

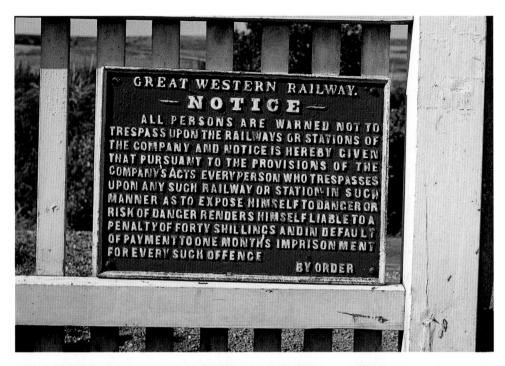

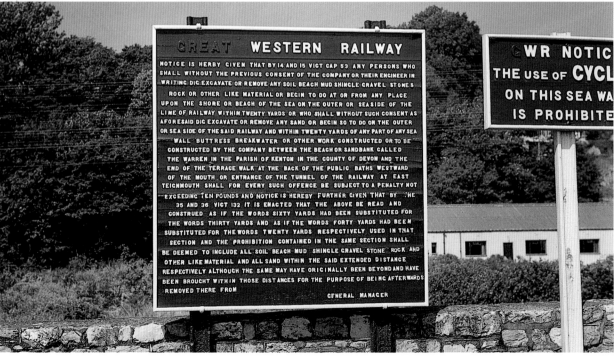

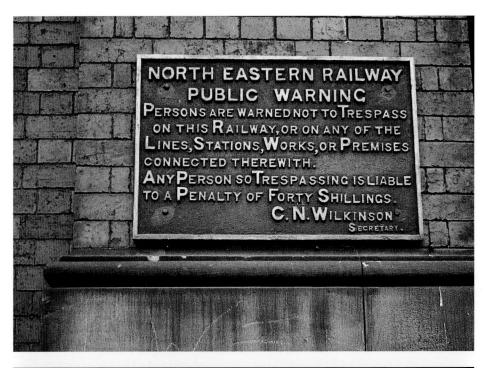

NORTH EASTERN RAILWAY
PUBLIC WARNING
PERSONS ARE WARNED NOT TO TRESPASS
ON THIS RAILWAY, OR ON ANY OF THE
LINES, STATIONS, WORKS, OR PREMISES
CONNECTED THEREWITH.
ANY PERSON SO TRESPASSING IS LIABLE
TO A PENALTY OF FORTY SHILLINGS.
C. N. WILKINSON
SECRETARY.

MOTOR CAR ACTS. 1896 AND 1903.
NOTICE.
THIS BRIDGE IS INSUFFICIENT TO CARRY A HEAVY MOTOR CAR
THE REGISTERED AXLE WEIGHT OF ANY AXLE OF WHICH EXCEEDS
THREE TONS, OR THE REGISTERED AXLE WEIGHTS OF THE
SEVERAL AXLES OF WHICH EXCEED IN THE AGGREGATE FIVE
TONS, OR A HEAVY MOTOR CAR DRAWING A TRAILER IF THE
REGISTERED AXLE WEIGHTS OF THE SEVERAL AXLES OF THE HEAVY
MOTOR CAR AND THE AXLE WEIGHTS OF THE SEVERAL AXLES OF
THE TRAILER EXCEED IN THE AGGREGATE FIVE TONS.
STRATFORD-ON-AVON.
MIDLAND JUNCTION RAILWAYS.
STRATFORD-ON-AVON.

SOMERSET AND DORSET JOINT LINE.
TRESPASSING ON THE RAILWAY.
NOTICE IS HEREBY GIVEN THAT UNDER THE PROVISIONS OF THE
37TH SECTION OF THE SOUTH WESTERN RAILWAY ACT, 1902, ANY
PERSON WHO SHALL TRESPASS UPON ANY OF THE LINES OF
RAILWAY BELONGING OR LEASED TO OR WORKED BY THE
SOUTH WESTERN RAILWAY COMPANY IN CONJUNCTION WITH
THE MIDLAND RAILWAY COMPANY, SHALL ON CONVICTION
BE LIABLE TO A PENALTY NOT EXCEEDING 40/- & PUBLIC
WARNING IS HEREBY GIVEN TO PERSONS NOT TO TRESPASS
UPON THE RAILWAY.
DATED THIS 5TH DAY OF AUGUST 1903
GODFREY KNIGHT,
WILLIAM CLOWER,   JOINT SECRETARIES.

S. & D.J.R.
BEWARE OF
TRAINS

Southern Region

There is no doubt that, on appointment as Chief Mechanical Engineer, Oliver Bulleid found the Southern Railway's steam power at a particularly low ebb, and that critical remarks made by him at the time were fully justified. Bulleid soon designed a powerful Pacific class of locomotive for use on the Eastern and Western sections, of which 30 examples were built at Eastleigh Works between 1941 and 1949. Thirty-five boilers were provided for the class, 10 being supplied under contract by the North British Locomotive Co, 13 were constructed at Eastleigh, and the remainder at Brighton Works. The class was designated

'Merchant Navy', with all carrying the names of shipping lines. Here, at Stewarts Lane depot on 10 May 1959, we see the first of the class which was originally numbered 21C1 and named *Channel Packet*, having left the erecting shop at Eastleigh Works on 17 February 1941. Renumbered 35001 by BR in October 1949, the locomotive was rebuilt in August 1959 and withdrawn in November 1964, having completed 1,095,884 miles in service. It is interesting to note that the original cost of building the locomotive was £23,840, while a nameplate from one of these engines sold at auction today would fetch far in excess of that figure!

Bulleid also designed a further class of lighter-weight Pacific locomotives, which were known as the 'West Country' and 'Battle of Britain' classes, although there were no technical differences between the two. A total of 110 were constructed: 104 at Brighton Works and six at Eastleigh Works. Dick was always welcome at Stewarts Lane and subjects were often moved into better locations to obtain the best photograph, and sometimes smoke was requested! Here we see No 34091 *Weymouth* beautifully prepared, ready to haul the 'Golden Arrow' from Victoria to Dover on 27 October 1957.

Rebuilt 'Merchant Navy' class No 35008 *Orient Line* pulls away from Seaton Junction with an up express from Exeter to Waterloo on 11 July 1959. This locomotive emerged from Eastleigh Works in June 1942 and covered 1,318,765 miles (the highest mileage of any 'Merchant Navy') before being withdrawn in July 1967, having survived to the end of steam on the Western Section of the Southern Region. Cutting up was carried out by J. Buttigieg of Newport soon after withdrawal.

A scene that is quite different today, with an office block above the station, Cannon Street is seen here on 31 May 1958, shortly before the overall roof was removed. Rebuilt 'West County' class 4-6-2 No 34025 *Whimple* departs with the 5.14pm service to Ramsgate via the London, Chatham & Dover main line.

Whimple was completed at Brighton Works in March 1946, rebuilt at Eastleigh in November 1957, and survived to the end of steam on the Southern Region, being withdrawn in July 1967. It was recorded working the 6.54pm from Waterloo to Basingstoke, two days before the final steam workings.

LEFT: Battle of Britain' class 4-6-2 No 34069 *Hawkinge* takes water at Yeovil Junction on 22 July 1958. These locomotives were mainly used on passenger services, but as in the photograph, they were sometimes used on mixed freight duties, in this case working west towards Exeter. *Hawkinge* was named after an RAF Battle of Britain fighter airfield in Kent and it entered traffic in October 1947. Withdrawn in November 1963, the recorded mileage in service was only 673,643.

ABOVE: Rebuilt 'Merchant Navy' class 4-6-2 No 35015 *Rotterdam Lloyd* approaches Factory Junction, Battersea, on the down 'Golden Arrow' from Victoria to Dover Marine. Not only did Dick have a good relationship with the staff at Stewarts Lane depot, but this obviously also applied to the signalmen at Factory Junction signalbox from which this photograph was taken 21 March 1959. It is interesting to note that Battersea Power Station was in operation at this time. *Rotterdam Lloyd* was completed at Eastleigh Works in March 1945, rebuilt there in June 1958, and was the first of the class to be withdrawn, in February 1964, having completed 813,950 miles in service. It is worth noting that a good number of Bulleid Pacifics have been preserved.

The three-cylinder 'Schools' class 4-4-0s of 1930–5 were without doubt the finest passenger locomotives designed by Maunsell and were able to haul all but the heaviest expresses on the Southern Railway. They were considered to be the most powerful 4-4-0s in Europe. All were named after public schools and here we see

No 30936 *Cranleigh* passing Denmark Hill station with a down relief from Victoria to Ramsgate, via the Catford loop on 16 May 1959. The very ornate station and signalbox were built jointly by the LBSCR and LCDR in 1865.

'Schools' class No 30925 *Cheltenham* is seen at Merstham on the Railway Correspondence & Travel Society special the 'Sussex Special' railtour on 7 October 1962. The RCTS has two proud boasts: it organised and ran the first railtour in 1938, and was the influence that resulted in the preservation of *Cheltenham* as part of the National Collection, and which can now be seen in the National Railway Museum at York.

A beautiful portrait of 'Schools' class No 30914 *Eastbourne* at Stewarts Lane depot on 24 May 1958. It is in British Railways lined-black livery retaining the early BR crest. This locomotive was built at Eastleigh Works in December 1932, the 40 locomotives of this class being specially designed with sloping cab sides and tenders for use on the Hastings line, which had several narrow tunnels. *Eastbourne* was one of four that was never repainted in green livery by BR, remaining in black until withdrawn, in July 1961. It was cut up at Ashford Works in September 1961.

Maunsell-designed 'Lord Nelson' class 4-6-0 No 30861 *Lord Anson* passes Kennington Junction, Oxford, with a Newcastle–Poole express on 15 August 1959. *Lord Anson* was built at Eastleigh Works in September 1929 and withdrawn in October 1962, being one of the last of the class in service. Fortunately, No 850 *Lord Nelson* survives as part of the National Collection and is currently in main line use, representing the 16-strong class.

King Arthur' class 4-6-0 No 30453 *King Arthur* in beautiful condition stands in the yard at Nine Elms shed on 6 September 1958. The Maunsell 'King Arthurs' were developed from the Urie-designed 'N15' class built between 1918 and 1923 (Nos 736-755). The modernisation of these engines was the work of Maunsell's design team at Eastleigh which was under the direction of the ex-Ashford Works team based at the SR's Waterloo headquarters. Ten engines (Nos 448–457) were built at Eastleigh Works in 1925, 30 (Nos 763–792) were delivered from the North British Locomotive Co the same year, and the final batch (Nos 793–806) was built at Eastleigh in 1926/7. Unfortunately, *King Arthur* did not survive into preservation, being withdrawn in July 1961, but class-mate No 30777 *Sir Lamiel* can be seen working on the main line today, being part of the National Collection.

Working away from Southern metals, 'King Arthur' class No 30782 *Sir Brian* stands in Oxford station on 29 September 1956. Great Western 'Modified Hall' class 4-6-0 No 6980 *Llanrumney Hall* had worked the York–Bournemouth service to Oxford and the Southern engine would take it forward to Bournemouth. From Dick's diary of Saturday 29 September 1956, he observed 52 different locomotives in a 4-hour period, and noted that Driver Watts of Bournemouth depot had worked up from his home shed; no doubt he would have driven the return duty! Note the wheeltapper standing on the track!

LEFT: Dick had photographers' good fortune to get two trains together at Bickley on 5 August 1957 as 'King Arthur' class No 30767 *Sir Valence* working the down 'Kentish Belle' overhauls a rather dirty and labouring Ashford-built 'N' class 2-6-0, No 31404, on a down excursion bound for Ramsgate. The signalbox and signals were swept away when the London–Chatham line was electrified in June 1959.

RIGHT: Douglas Earle Marsh designed the London, Brighton & South Coast Railway Atlantics. These were based on Great Northern Railway, Doncaster drawings with certain useful alterations. Two batches of locomotives were built, the first five ('H1' class) in 1905/6 by Kitson of Leeds, and the second six ('H2' class) at Brighton Works in 1911. Here, we see 'H2' No 32424 *Beachy Head* at Star Lane on the Quarry line heading the RCTS's 'Sussex Coast Limited' railtour from Victoria to Newhaven on 13 April 1958. This was the final run of *Beachy Head*, which was withdrawn shortly after the tour, having completed 1,090,661 miles in 47 years of service. A full-size working replica of this locomotive is under construction on the Bluebell Railway.

BELOW: In 1913, Robert Billinton designed a 2-6-0 locomotive for the LBSCR, classified 'K'. Seventeen locomotives, costing £3,150 each, were built at Brighton Works between September 1913 and March 1921. No 32342 is seen here near Selsdon on 11 May 1958 on a ramblers' excursion Bluebell Special, from Greenford to Haywards Heath. The Mogul worked the special from East Croydon via Oxted and East Grinstead to Haywards Heath. The whole class was withdrawn at the end of 1962, and none survive.

'King Arthur' class 4-6-0 No 30796 *Sir Dodinas le Savage* departs from Brighton on the return RCTS special the 'Sussex Coast Limited', bound for Victoria. (See the earlier Brighton Atlantic photograph for the outward leg of this tour.) No 30796 was built at Eastleigh Works in May 1926 and was fitted for use on the Brighton section with a six-wheel tender, owing to weight restrictions, the coal capacity being limited to 2½ tons and water to 3,300 gallons. It was withdrawn in February 1962.

'H15' class 4-6-0 No 30491 leaves Hinton Admiral in the New Forest, with an up passenger train from Bournemouth on 28 June 1957. The class was designed by Robert Urie and built at Eastleigh Works, this locomotive appearing in May 1914, surviving until February 1961. The carriage stock, set No 243, is of interest, being of Maunsell design and painted in 'plum and spilt milk' livery. The 4-6-0 was allocated to the Western Section of the Southern Region for local services between Weymouth, Bournemouth and Southampton and was withdrawn in November 1959. The camping coach in the yard is of interest.

Urie's third, final and improved 4-6-0 design, the goods 'S15' class, was introduced in 1920. When the Southern Railway required additional heavy goods locomotives for work on the Western Section, Maunsell modified Urie's original design, as seen here with No 30824 on a pick-up freight at Broad Clyst on 6 July 1961. It was built at Eastleigh Works in March 1927 and survived until September 1965. The modified class of 15 locomotives introduced in 1927 cost £10,415 each; a further batch of 10 with a few further detailed modifications was built in 1936.

RIGHT: 'U1' class 2-6-0 No 31897 in good clean condition heads an up empty stock-working at St Mary Cray Junction on 16 May 1959. Set No 233 comprises standard Maunsell-designed coaches. The track layout was in the process of being widened to four lines, ready for the commencement of the Kent Coast electrification. The signal and signalbox on the right of the photograph were soon to be swept away when the new colour-light system was introduced.

BELOW: A rather dirty 'N' class 2-6-0, No 31854, rounds the curve at Shortlands Junction with an up train from the Kent coast on 2 August 1958. The locomotive was part-built by Woolwich Arsenal and completed at Ashford Works in March 1925. It was withdrawn from service in June 1964.

RIGHT: Not perhaps the ideal locomotive for freight work, the Drummond 'T9' class 4-4-0s were known as 'Greyhounds' for their turn of speed with their 6ft 7in driving wheels. The 66 locomotives of the class were built between 1899 and 1901 for the London & South Western Railway, with construction shared between Dubs & Co and Nine Elms Works. The example shown, No 30289, was built in 1900 and was withdrawn in November 1959. The crew poses for Dick's camera on a beautiful sunny day at Brockenhurst on 28 June 1957; no doubt they received a print.

BELOW: Seen at the end of the former LSW line at Padstow on 15 July 1960, 'T9' class No 30719 blows off gently while shunting stock to form a train to Okehampton. No 30719 was built by Dubs in 1899 and was withdrawn in March 1961. Fortunately, one member of the class survived into preservation, No 30120, now part of the National Collection, recently moved from the Bluebell Railway to Bodmin & Wenford Railway.

H. S. Wainwright designed the handsome 'D' class 4-4-0s for the South Eastern & Chatham Railway, this one fittingly photographed at its place of construction, Ashford Works, where it was completed in December 1901. Beautifully restored to original livery by the Ashford Works staff, No 737 waits in the works yard on 20 June 1960 before being moved to the Transport Museum at Clapham. Following the closure of that museum, the locomotive was transferred to the National Railway Museum at York.

Ex-SECR Wainwright 'L' class 4-4-0s Nos 31760 and 31768 pass Gipsy Hill with an excursion from Victoria to Robertsbridge for the Kent & East Sussex Railway on 18 October 1959. An interesting note in the RCTS magazine, *The Railway Observer*, of the time states: 'By dint of scraping the barrel, a ten-coach train was got together consisting of eight Hastings-gauge corridors, green-painted Pullman buffet car No 182 and just seen here, a SECR ten-compartment second, quite a long journey in this coach without any facilities!'

This was the last day of the steam-hauled 'Night Ferry', with the up train seen passing Sydenham Hill on 13 June 1959, hauled by 'L1' class 4-4-0 No 31753 and 'Battle of Britain' class 4-6-2 No 34068 *Kenley*. The weight of the train, which included Wagons Lits sleeping cars, usually necessitated two locomotives. Dick has coped really well with this shot as the train, due in Victoria at about 9am, always had to be photographed against the light.

ABOVE: It was a sad occasion on 4 November 1961 when the last 'D1' class 4-4-0, No 31749, and the last 'E1' class 4-4-0, No 31067, worked their final run to Ashford Works for cutting up, and are seen at Bat & Ball, Sevenoaks. Both locomotives were in a very clean condition for their final turn, the 10.10am from Stewarts Lane hauling an inspection saloon to Sevenoaks, then heading the 12.2pm ballast train from Bat & Ball to Tonbridge, finally running light to Ashford. Before the days of email and text messages, any information of an unusual working was passed to photographers by letter or telephone. A copy of the letter containing the final working information is reproduced on this page; an amazing record! Dick Hardy comments: 'If any engine should have been preserved it was an "E1" such as 31019'. Many would echo that thought.

LEFT: This is all that remains of 'D1' No 31749: the Beyer Peacock works plate, rebuilt 1921, now safely preserved. *Rodney Lissenden*

BRITISH RAILWAYS   BRITISH TRANSPORT COMMISSION

SOUTHERN REGION   South Eastern Division

T. R. V. BOLLAND Line Traffic Manager
R. SHERVINGTON Traffic Superintendent
J. K. BLUE Freight Commercial Officer

2. 11. 61.

Dear Mr Harvey,

You will probably be interested, to say the least, to hear that on Tuesday 31st Oct, 31739 ran light at 1.00 am from B. Arms to Ashford, + was followed 24 hours later by 31489.

Also, this coming Saturday, 4th Nov., at 10-10am from Stewarts Lane, Inspection saloon DS1 is being hauled via Brixton, Beckenham Jn, a Orpington to Sevenoaks by 31749 a 31067. The engines then run light from Sevenoaks to Bat & Ball to work a 12.2pm ballast to Tonbridge, arriving at 12.30pm. Thence they go light engines 12.54pm to Ashford arriving at 1.50pm

Another Urie design, the 'G16' class 4-8-0Ts were constructed at Eastleigh Works in 1921 especially to work the hump yard at Feltham and short-distance freights in London. There were only four of the class built, at a cost of £9,536 apiece. No 30495 is seen here at Feltham shed on 17 October 1959. It was withdrawn in December 1962, having covered the surprisingly high mileage of 803,887.

A Urie design for the London & South Western Railway, the 'H16' class 4-6-2Ts, a class of five locomotives introduced in 1921 to work the cross-London freight services from the hump yard at Feltham. No 30517 is seen in Wimbledon yard taking water on the occasion of the RCTS/SLS railtour on 2 December 1962.

The Southern Railway required a large tank locomotive for working cross-London freights and so the 'W' class 2-6-4Ts, which were effectively tank-engine versions of the 'N1' Class 2-6-0s, were produced. Maunsell authorised the construction of 15 locomotives, Nos 1911 to 1915, which were built at Eastleigh Works in 1932, and Nos 1916 to 1925 completed at Ashford Works in 1935/6. No 31925 was recorded at Hither Green depot on 28 February 1960. After 27 years in service, it was withdrawn in November 1963 and cut up at Eastleigh. None survive.

Constructed at Brighton Works in 1929, the Maunsell-designed 'Z' class 0-8-0Ts cost £6,145 per locomotive. Designed for shunting and heavy local freight working, the eight locomotives in the class were all withdrawn by the end of 1962 and broken up. Seen at Exmouth Junction shed is the first of the class, No 30950, shunting wagons on 5 July 1961.

ABOVE: Although quite a rural scene, this is only a few miles from the centre of London. Ex-South Eastern & Chatham Railway Wainwright-designed 'C' class 0-6-0 No 31717 ambles through Denmark Hill station with the 5.40pm empty stock-working from Rotherhithe Road to Cannon Street to form the 6.24pm working to Dover on 6 May 1959, on this occasion running via Blackheath and Ludgate Hill.

RIGHT: Former SECR 'O1' class 0-6-0 No 31258 arrives at Shepherdswell with a Railway Enthusiasts Club special to the East Kent Railway on 23 May 1958. A light freight locomotive built at Ashford Works in May 1894, and rebuilt in May 1914, No 31258 was one of the last members of the class to be withdrawn, being condemned in February 1961. Owing to their light axle loading, two members of the class were retained to work in the Kent coalfield and around the Dover Harbour area. No 31065 is preserved and restored in SECR livery as No.65, and can be seen on the Bluebell Railway.

Built for the London, Brighton &
South Coast Railway, the 'C2' class
and rebuilt 'C2X' class 0-6-0s were
designed by Robert Billinton and
built by Vulcan Foundry between
1892 and 1902. No 32449 was
recorded at Brighton shed on
13 April 1958 and was withdrawn
from service in June 1961. Another
class with no survivors.

No 30694, photographed at Nine
Elms shed on 6 September 1958,
was one of the '700' class 0-6-0
locomotives built for the London &
South Western Railway to the
design of Dugald Drummond. All
30 of the class were built by Dubs
& Co between March and August
1897 at a cost of £2,695 per
locomotive and the whole class was
withdrawn by the end of 1962.

In August 1940, Bulleid recommended to the Southern Railway the construction of some heavy duty 0-6-0 locomotives. The austere appearance was to surprise many people when the first 'Q1' class appeared in March 1942. A total of 40 locomotives were built over a 12-month period at Brighton and Ashford works. A remarkably clean No 33015 was photographed at Nine Elms shed on 6 September 1958. The final locomotive of the class was withdrawn in September 1965, but fortunately the first of the class built, No C1, later 33001, is preserved in the National Collection.

After the production of the 'Schools' class in 1935, the Southern Railway reduced the funds allotted for steam construction, as the directors wished to reserve resources for main line electrification. However, a large number of worn-out machines needed to be replaced and by January 1938 it was decided to build the 'Q' class 0-6-0s. Designed by Maunsell, but introduced into traffic by Bulleid, 20 locomotives were built at Eastleigh Works between January 1938 and September 1939. The final member of the class, No 30549, is shown here at Norwood Junction shed in its ultimate form, fitted with BR Class 4-type blast pipe and a small stove-pipe chimney, which improved steaming and reduced coal consumption, but not appearance.

RIGHT: H' class 0-4-4T No 31542 poses in front of the well-known landmark building at Stewarts Lane shed on 10 September 1958. This class was very popular on the various branch lines in the southeast, and many were fitted for push-pull working. In total, 64 were built at Ashford Works between 1905 and 1909, plus a final two in 1915. No 31542 was withdrawn in November 1962. One of the class, No 263, has survived into preservation, and at the time of writing, is undergoing overhaul on the Bluebell Railway.

BELOW: 'R1' class 0-6-0T No 31337 rests in front of Folkestone Junction signalbox on 18 October 1958. James Stirling introduced the 'R' class to the South Eastern Railway in 1888, a total of 25 being built at Ashford Works, of which 13 were later rebuilt and classified 'R1'. These all survived into BR days, mainly owing to their work on the Whitstable Harbour branch and banking duties on the Folkestone Harbour branch. There were many alterations to those locomotives that worked through the low Tyler Hill Tunnel to Whitstable, including cut-down chimneys and rounded cabs to fit through the small bore. No 31337 remained at Folkestone as standby engine until withdrawn in February 1960.

RIGHT: Wainwright designed the rather attractive 'P' class 0-6-0T for the SECR, all eight of which were built at Ashford Works in 1909/10, at a cost of £1,740 each. The very pleasing design of the Wainwright pagoda-style cab was also fitted to many other locomotives, including 'H', 'J' and 'R1' classes. The 'Ps' remained in service for many years, mainly owing to their short wheelbase and the ability to work where other classes were not allowed. No 31558 stands in front of part of the former Longhedge Works on 20 October 1958. Four of the class have been preserved and can be seen on the Bluebell and Kent & East Sussex railways.

ABOVE: William Adams designed this very handsome 4-4-2T locomotive (later known as Class 0415), for the LSWR. Locomotives were constructed by Robert Stephenson, Dubs, Beyer Peacock and Neilson, between 1882 and 1885. Of the 71 built, all bar 3 were withdrawn by 1927, this trio soldiering on until 1961. Two of the class (original numbers 125 and 520) survived solely for working the Lyme Regis branch, while No 488 was sold in 1917 to the Ministry of Munitions and then to the East Kent Railway. It was purchased by the Southern Railway in March 1946 to strengthen the class employed on the Devon–Dorset branch line. After withdrawal, No 488, as BR No 30583, was purchased by the Bluebell Railway with much advice and help from Dick Riley (see Introduction). Photographed leaving Combpyne en route to Lyme Regis, sister locomotive No 30584 hauls a single Maunsell coach on 8 July 1959.

LEFT: An interesting view of Adams '0415' class 4-4-2T No 30582 in ex-works condition, standing in the yard at Exmouth Junction shed on 15 July 1960, specially prepared for the LSWR centenary exhibition at Exeter four days later. This is one of the three locomotives that survived the demise of the rest of the class in the 1920s, as detailed above, to service the Axminster–Lyme Regis branch.

LSWR Class O2 0-4-4T No 30193 stands at St Budeaux on 28 August 1961. This class of 60 locomotives was built at Nine Elms Works between 1889 and 1895 to the design of William Adams for work on lighter suburban services and rural branch lines. Later, 23 members of the class served on the Isle of Wight, having been transferred from the mainland, between 1925 and 1949. All were modified with extended bunkers, Westinghouse air brakes, fitted with hooters, and were numbered W14 to W36 and given names of places on the island. No 30193, which remained on the mainland, was withdrawn from service in April 1962.

Nine Elms Works built all 34 of the 'G6' class 0-6-0Ts between 1894 and 1900. They spent the majority of their working lives on the Western Section of the Southern, being based at ten different sheds. No 30349 is seen in the yard of Feltham shed on 19 March 1961, a few months before withdrawal from service.

A very clean Drummond 'M7' class 0-4-4T, No 30060, is recorded with its push-pull set of LSWR stock, leaving Brockenhurst on 28 June 1957. This local train will take the Ringwood loop en route to Bournemouth. All but 10 of the class of 105 locomotives were built at Nine Elms Works between 1897 and 1911, at a cost of £1,445 apiece. The remaining 10 were completed at Eastleigh Works at a cost of £1,715 each. During their many years of service, this very successful class could be seen over the whole of the Southern Railway and Region. No 30060 was withdrawn in July 1961 but is survived by Nos 30053, preserved on the Swanage Railway, and 245, in the National Collection.

Adams 'B4' class 0-4-0T No 30093, introduced by the LSWR in 1891, outshedded from Eastleigh to Winchester, shunts the yard there on 5 March 1960. These small tank-locomotives were designed for service in docks and on station pilot duties, with 25 constructed between 1892 and 1908. No 30093 was withdrawn in April 1960, having covered 479,705 miles in its lifetime, an amazing total for such a small engine. Two examples survive, at the Bluebell Railway and Bressingham Steam Museum.

Beattie '0298' class 2-4-0WT No 30586 at its home town of Wadebridge. This is a story of survival, similar to the '0415' class, in that 85 engines were built (by Beyer Peacock) between 1863 and 1875, with all withdrawn except for three which survived into British Railways days for use on a specific duty. They were found to be the only locomotives suitable to work the china-clay trains over the Wenford Bridge mineral line in Cornwall. The three were withdrawn in December 1962, but fortunately two have survived into preservation with both recently returned to working order.

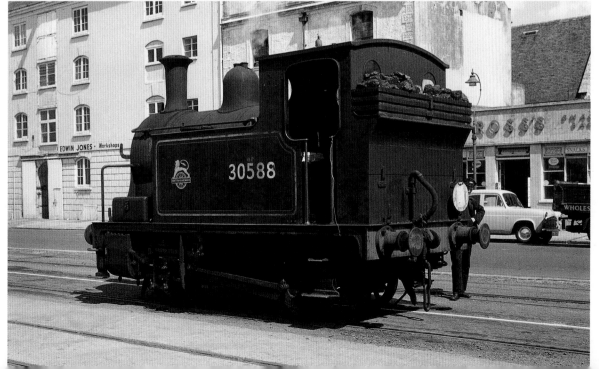

The diminutive LSWR Class C14 0-4-0T, No 30588, is seen in the street in the vicinity of the Royal Pier at Southampton on 26 June 1957. The class of ten engines had originally been designed as 2-2-0s in 1906 for use on rail motor services, but were found to have difficulties with adhesion owing to their non-coupled wheels. By 1914, they were converted to 0-4-0Ts, and seven were subsequently sold for wartime service, but three survived into Nationalisation, receiving BR numbers. No 30588 was withdrawn in December 1957.

LBSCR 'A1X' class 0-6-0T No 32650 approaches Langston station on a train from Havant to Hayling Island on 2 November 1963. The train is crowded as this was the final day of service on the branch. The restricted weight permitted on this line was one of the reasons why the Brighton 'Terriers' lasted well into British Railways days and of the original 50, 13 received BR numbers. No 32650 was built as an 'A1' at Brighton Works in December 1876, rebuilt as 'A1X' in 1920, and withdrawn from traffic in November 1963. Fortunately, no fewer than ten of the class survived into preservation, including one in Canada. No 32650 can be seen today on the Spa Valley Railway at Tunbridge Wells.

A very clean Brighton 'Terrier' in Stroudley LBSCR livery, No 377s, acting as Brighton Works shunter, is seen at Brighton shed on 23 June 1956. Built as an 'A1' in June 1878 as LBSCR No 35, rebuilt as 'A1X' in 1922, renumbered 635, it became SR No 2635 and passed into departmental stock as No 377s in August 1946, later numbered DS377. The locomotive was returned to capital stock as BR No 32635 in January 1959, it was withdrawn in March 1963, and broken up that September.

Another of Stroudley's 'Terriers', No 82 *Boxhill,* is seen at Brighton shed on 13 April 1958. *Boxhill* was displayed at the Waterloo centenary celebrations in 1948 and at various other exhibitions until it was moved into store at Tweedmouth shortly after this photograph was taken. The locomotive was eventually moved to Eastleigh Works for refurbishment and then put on display at Clapham Museum. It can now be seen at the National Railway Museum at York.

The 'E1/R' class 0-6-2Ts were a rebuild of the LBSCR 'E1' 0-6-0Ts. In 1927, the Southern Railway decided that there was a requirement for larger tank-locomotives for use in the West Country and ten 'E1s' were rebuilt at Brighton with longer frames, enlarged bunkers and additional water capacity. Smartly turned out No 32697, with early BR crest, is seen at Exeter St Davids awaiting its next turn of duty on 28 June 1957.

LBSCR 'E2' class 0-6-0T No 32106 is seen at Stewarts Lane shed on 1 March 1959. The class of ten locomotives was designed by L. B. Billinton and built at Brighton Works between June 1913 and October 1916. The delay in the construction of such a small class was due to the disruption caused by World War One. The final five locomotives received larger water tanks. No 32106 was withdrawn in October 1962, having completed 725,090 miles. Dick Hardy reports that the 'E2s' were highly regarded as shunting engines by the staff at Stewarts Lane.

Robert Billinton designed the 'E4' class 0-6-2Ts for both passenger and goods duties, a total of 75 being built at Brighton Works between December 1897 and September 1903. No 32508, originally named *Bognor*, rests in the yard of Brighton shed on 13 April 1958. It survived the cutter's torch until April 1963.

The date of Dick's photograph was the occasion of the RCTS farewell tour to the Brighton Atlantic *Beachy Head*. How 'health & safety' would have coped today with the complete train load of enthusiasts descending on the shed is left to the imagination!

Four of the 'E4s' were reboilered in 1909 and 1911 to become the 'E4X' class. Both the diameter and length of the boiler were extended by about three inches and the overall weight increased by nearly seven tons. In Brighton days, they appeared to work more than their fair share of goods duties, as well as frequently spending quite lengthy periods yard-shunting. No 32477 stands between a 'C2X' and an 'E6' at Norwood Junction shed on 12 April 1958, eight months before withdrawal.

Another attractive Billinton large tank engine, the 'E6' class 0-6-2Ts, comprised a total of 12 locomotives built at Brighton Works in 1904/5. No 32418, seen here at Norwood Junction shed on 12 April 1958, was one of the final three to be withdrawn in December 1962. Robert Billinton died in November 1904 and it was left to Douglas Earle Marsh to complete the delivery of the class, the major change being the first ten were delivered in Stroudley goods green, whereas the final two left the works in Marsh black livery.

An LMS design by Ivatt, dating from 1946, was the '2MT' class. These 2-6-2Ts were introduced on BR Southern Region, as many of the original tank engines designed for branch lines had come to the end of their useful lives.. Here we see No 41306 about to depart Exmouth on the branch train to Exeter on 13 October 1959. A few years earlier this train would have been worked by an LSWR 'M7' class 0-4-4T.

The now-preserved Ivatt 2-6-2T No 41312 leaves Meeth Halt with a single coach, forming the service from Torrington to Halwill Junction on 25 September 1962. The North Devon & Cornwall Junction Light Railway was built to serve a sparsely populated area as well as the clay works situated along the 19 miles of the branch. The famed Colonel H. F. Stephens was the operator of this light railway at one time, as he was of a number of lines in the southeast of England, including the East Kent and Kent & East Sussex railways. Passenger services on the West Country line ceased on 1 March 1965, followed by freight in September 1969.

British Railways Standard Class 2 2-6-2T No 84021 departs from Ramsgate with the service for Canterbury and Ashford on 28 March 1959. The locomotive was built at Darlington Works and delivered new to the Southern Region in June 1957. It remained on the Southern until June 1961 when it was transferred to the London Midland Region at Bedford. After only seven years in service it was withdrawn in June 1964 and cut up by J. Cashmore of Great Bridge, four months later.

Great credit should be given to Dick Riley for the way he recorded the passing scene, which not only included steam but other forms of traction. This classic view shows '4-SUB' EMU No 4506 in Clapham Cutting en route to Waterloo on 24 May 1958. The unit comprises early LBSCR vintage coaches originally built for the overhead wire AC electric services which ran between 1912 and 1924. No 4506 was condemned in December 1959.

Another most interesting picture! Oliver Bulleid, famed for his Pacifics, also designed a double-deck EMU, only two sets of which were built in 1949, Nos 4001 and 4002. The first of these is seen here entering Cannon Street on 12 June 1959. There was considered to be a need to increase the seating capacity of the normal '4-SUB' EMUs from 468 to accommodate more passengers, and these units carried 552. The working life of these two units was spent in north Kent based at Slade Green depot. They were not regarded as being very successful and in their later years were restricted to rush-hour services, but despite being non-standard were not withdrawn until October 1971.

In the days of an overall roof at Cannon Street, new 'Hastings' diesel-electric multiple unit No 1017 leaves on the 5.15pm service to Hastings on 30 May 1958. British Railways introduced the new design of multiple units specifically for use on this line and they were therefore built with narrow bodies because of the restricted width of the tunnels on this route. They had English Electric 500hp power units, two to a 6-coach train. When the Hastings line was electrified the units became redundant but several vehicles were preserved and are now run on the main line by Hastings Diesels Ltd.

Still steam! Paddle steamer *Princess Elizabeth* approaches Ryde Pier on 25 May 1957; Dick obviously could not resist this shot while on a trip to the Isle of Wight. *Princes Elizabeth* was built by Day, Summers & Co at Northam and launched on 2 June 1927. It had an interesting career, including conversion to a minesweeper in 1939. Now preserved and currently at Dunkirk, it is used as a floating restaurant.

Many of Dick's early railway visits would have started from Tulse Hill, but from 1972 Beckenham became the starting point. Therefore, there is some licence for the two photographs on this page. A very fine LCDR signal gantry stands at the end of the up platform at Beckenham Junction, while the signalbox can be seen in the background. Both were swept away with the electrification of the Kent Coast line in 1959.

Dick photographed many buses and it was thought it would be a fitting reminder of his work that just one bus picture should appear! London Transport RT3254, one of a class of 4,825 'RTs', awaits departure from Beckenham Junction on route 54 to Croydon on 11 August 1977.

To end the book, what could be better than a photograph taken at the bottom of Dick's garden! The house in Albemarle Road, Beckenham, had previously been occupied by Kenneth Wightman, whose photographs many will know. Kenneth sold the house to Dick and Christine in 1972, rather too late for steam, but still a good location for more modern shots. Dick obviously spent a good amount of time with Ken at the end of the garden, as did the author! Here, 'Schools' class No 30913 *Christ's Hospital* approaches Shortlands Junction working a down Ramsgate service on 2 August 1958.